一位摄影师眼中的邓小平

Decisive Moments in History: Deng Xiaoping Through the Eyes of a Photographer

杨绍明　编著

Edited by Yang Shaoming

浙江人民美术出版社

邓小平同志是中国社会主义改革开放和现代化建设的总设计师，中国特色社会主义道路的开创者，邓小平理论的主要创立者。1992 年初，邓小平同志赴南方视察，他以一个伟大的马克思主义者的远见卓识，科学总结了中共十一届三中全会以来改革开放的基本实践和经验，发表了具有划时代意义的重要讲话，回答了长期以来困扰和束缚人们思想的许多重大认识问题，指导中国改革开放和社会主义现代化建设进入一个新阶段。

Comrade Deng Xiaoping is the chief architect of the socialist reform and opening-up in China, the driving force behind the country's modernization, the pioneer of building socialism with Chinese characteristics, and the principal founder of Deng Xiaoping Theory. As a true Marxist with great vision, he embarked on the historic southern tour in early 1992. In a series of talks that he delivered on the trip, he confirmed China's commitment to reform and opening-up by summarizing the lessons and experience the Communist Party of China (CPC) had gained since the 3rd Plenary Session of the 11th Central Committee. The tour and talks provided timely answers to many of the fundamental questions about China's reform and opening-up, while liberating people's minds from old ideas by giving them new confidence. The southern tour will forever be one of Deng Xiaoping's most enduring legacies, as it has revitalized China's reform and opening-up and launched the country's socialist modernization into a new phase.

序

骆飞

智慧点亮人生，同样，智慧也点亮艺术。

摄影家杨绍明用心、用情，努力将政治的、历史的、哲学的、文学的学习与理解融会贯通，化为摄影艺术创造的动力和智慧，定格时代，定格春秋，逐渐形成自己独特的艺术风格，当之无愧地成为中国摄影史上承前启后的代表人物之一。

日本新闻界朋友称他为“中国最著名的时政摄影家”。

的确，杨绍明的摄影艺术常常是与政治风云、时事要闻紧密相系的。了解他的人都发现，在他的身上，似乎比别人更多一些历史的和政治的基因。

杨绍明 1942 年出生于陕北延安。他生于战争岁月，长于中国革命摇篮，长期受家庭影响的人生之旅，决定了他对于政治风云的特殊敏感，对于政坛人物、重大事件的极大热情，而这一切无疑奠定了时政摄影的坚实根基。还有一个条件，他比别人似乎更容易切入重大活动，接近重要人物。当然，最重要的还是他自己的选择。早在学生时代，他就爱上了摄影，并且梦想当一名新闻记者。他选择的是，用人类的第三只眼睛——相机，来评古论今，谈天说地，舒卷风云。历经风雨，千磨万击，他终于练出了不凡的身手。

一名时政摄影家，既要具备新闻记者的职业敏感，又要有全面把握时事政局的宏观考虑；既要有关于社会、时政、历史等方面广博的文化知识的积累，又要对社会的因素有比较透彻的理解。在谈到这一点时，杨绍明说：“我真应该感谢我的父母，在迷上摄影并一心想当新闻记者的时候，是他们告诫我，没有较高的文化修养，是当不好记者的。要有相当的文化水平才行。”此后，杨绍明考入北京大学历史系，进行系统的学习深造。他深深地认识到，只有透彻地了解历史，才能更清楚地懂得今天，才会对当今和未来的时政有犀利的辨析。这正是他的代表作既有强烈的时代性，又具有深厚的历史感的原因。杨绍明是善于拍摄重要新闻人物和处理重大新闻事件报道的行家。他的新闻摄影，大气磅礴而又细致入微，人物形态分明，静中有动，内心世界隐约可见，在鲜活的现场感中，体现出丰富的历史感。

杨绍明作为一名时政摄影家，很大程度上又是同领袖人物联系在一起的。早在 20 世纪 50 年代，他就拍摄过毛泽东出访苏联、在十三陵水库参加劳动等珍贵照片。之后，还拍过周恩来、刘少奇、邓小平等领导人的活动。伴随着改革开放崭新历史时期的到来，杨绍明很自然地成为关注和表现中国改革开放总设计师邓小平的热心记者。拍摄邓小平，杨绍明不是唯一的一名摄影家，但就跨度而言，就深度而言，就表现中国改革开放总设计师邓小平的生动性而言，杨绍明是名列前茅者。从 1962 年至 1992 年，杨绍明为邓小平拍摄了大量珍贵照片。其中，既有表现邓小平伟大胸襟、豪迈气概和高风亮节的作品，又有反映邓小平平易近人、朴实无华、可亲可敬的作品，更有展示邓小平尽享天伦、充满人情味的作品。这些作品共同构成了一个既具丰厚美学意义，又有极强文献价值的伟人系列，不仅从不同侧面完整而又准确地刻画了一代伟人邓小平集伟大与平凡于一身、形神兼备、血肉丰满的形象，而且为当代中国波澜壮阔的历史提供了真实、形象、感人的见证。从中国经历了十年“文革”陷入困境，邓小平受命于危难之际，到大刀阔斧地进行全面整顿，从设计改革开放的宏伟蓝图，到退下来以后的学习、工作、生活——杨绍明既然选择了研究邓小平的职业，就毫不迟疑地将镜头对准邓小平，并努力使自己的作品出类拔萃。

杨绍明拍摄邓小平，不同于外国的摄影师。他十分崇拜摄影大师亨利・卡蒂埃－布列松（Henri Cartier-Bresson，1908—2004），将卡蒂埃－布列松“决定性瞬间”的理论巧妙地应用于时政摄影，常常在重要的时间、重要的地点、重要的事件中，抓住重要的“情节”，表达特殊的发现和选择，阐述重要的问题和理解。他还善于驾驭摄影语言的独特性，寓无形之理于有形之象，将艺术的感觉与哲学的思考在画面中整合起来，从而产生表面的冲击力和内在的张力。1992 年春，邓小平视察南方沿海开放城市，杨绍明以敏锐的目光和清醒的意识，抓住这个非同寻常的行程带来的时机，拍摄了邓小平视察时同各界群众水乳交融、信心百倍的生动镜头，这组意味深长的照片刚刚在国内重要报刊发表，立即引起强烈反响。人们不仅真切地感受到“南国春来早”的气息，而且充分体会到社会主义中国又一个崭新的春天的到来。

杨绍明拍摄邓小平，也不同于国内许多新闻机构的摄影记者。他善于把邓小平当作一位爱国爱民、造福后代的情感丰富的长者来观察、来理解、来表现，突破了领袖人物正襟危坐、高不可攀的传统模式，除去了领袖人物头上的光环，置伟人于群众之中、生活之中、妻子儿女之中，在生活的实处把伟人与普通人统一起来，把形与神统一起来。1980 年的一幅《乡情》，捕捉到邓小平“人民公仆”的真实形象，传递了伟人质朴无华的情感。他的这种“还神为人”的愿望实现了。1988 年，杨绍明的系列照片《退下来以后的邓小平》在荷兰第 31 届世界新闻摄影比赛中获奖，实现了中国摄影师在“荷赛”的“零的突破”。这组照片赢得了世界同行的普遍认同。这也是杨绍明时政摄影生涯中的一个重要里程碑。杨绍明无疑是表现领袖人物有突破、有建树的代表人物之一。

杨绍明认为，摄影是科技发展的产物，当今的崭新科技又为摄影的发展提供了最大可能，只有更好地掌握技艺技巧，才能最大限度地发挥自己的潜能。他不仅在光线造型、瞬间捕捉等方面功力独具、胜人一筹，而且常常能在各种不利条件下化被动为主动，变不能为有所作为。他曾在光线极微弱的情况下，手持相机胸有成竹地拍下不可多得的精彩瞬间；他也曾在飞速奔驰的火车上探出身子拍下无法停车拍摄的重要场景；他曾在灯光交错、令人眼花缭乱的新闻现场快速扫描，抓到“独家新闻”；他也曾在众人都束手无策的情况下获得意想不到的成功——娴熟的技艺技巧不仅为杨绍明时政摄影最终目的的实现提供有效保证，而且使得他的追求显现出耐人寻味的个性色彩。

杨绍明是中国当代著名的摄影家，正如作家柯灵对他评价的那样：摄影家穿越浩瀚无际的时空，用超人的敏锐、准确、识力与果断，寻求选择创造对象，在最重要的场合，最关键的时刻，用最恰当的角度，按下快门，在闪电式的奇袭中，使瞬间化为永恒。

一幅优秀的摄影作品，不仅会给人以审美愉悦，而且还会给人以感染力和启迪，甚至达到振聋发聩的效果。就像一棵树摇动另一棵树，一朵云推动另一朵云，一个灵魂唤醒另一个灵魂，杨绍明用一幅幅作品记录历史、记录时代，不仅彰显了摄影的重要价值和无穷魅力，而且为中国摄影史留下了点亮征程的路标。

FOREWORD

Luo Fei

Wisdom enlightens art, in the same way it enlightens life.

Yang Shaoming has surely earned a rightful place as one of the Chinese photography's leading figures with his influential works. Focusing on the great changes in modern China, his unique artistic style as a photographer finds its motivation and inspiration from his heart and soul, from a lifetime of learning about politics, history, philosophy and literature and understanding their connections.

He was fondly referred to by his friends in the Japanese press as "the most famous political news photographer in China".

Indeed, Yang Shaoming's photography is often intertwined with political vicissitudes and current affairs, and this comes as no surprise to anyone familiar with his life story.

Born in Yan'an of Northern Shaanxi in 1942, Yang Shaoming was raised in the cradle of the Chinese revolution during times of war. Given the great influence of his family, it was only natural for him to grow up with a unique curiosity towards the world of politics, as well as a lifelong passion for following political leaders and major events. Actually, one might argue that Yang Shaoming was born to become a master of news photography. He also enjoyed the rare privilege of having close access to the men and women who made history. What mattered the most, of course, was his own choice. He fell in love with photography as early as his school days, and dreamed about becoming a journalist ever since. It was his own choice in life to pick up the camera, using its lens as his "third eye", to capture decisive moments in history and tell great stories. Through years of hard work and perfecting his skills, he has finally become an accomplished photographer.

It is no easy feat to become a great political news photographer, as it requires both a professional journalist's sensitivity and a general consideration of the larger social and political context. It also requires broad knowledge of history and politics, as well as an acute understanding of social changes. In this regard, Yang Shaoming attributed his achievement to the teaching of his parents. "I really have my parents to thank for this. They taught me the importance of obtaining a good education when I first dreamed about becoming a photojournalist, and they urged me to get one." The good education that Yang Shaoming had acquired from Peking University has certainly contributed to his photographic masterpieces, which reflect both the zeitgeist of the day and a strong sense of the past. A thorough appreciation of history leads to a better comprehension of the present, which in turn leads to the insightful analysis of the latest political events. As a master photographer who specializes in taking pictures of celebrities and major news events, Yang Shaoming has received wide acclaim for his photojournalism, which achieves a balance between magnificence and meticulousness. His works are especially famous for the way he depicts his human subjects, as he manages to reveal their inner worlds through the careful juxtaposition of history and the present.

Yang Shaoming's career as a news photographer is largely associated with China's leaders. As early as the 1950s, he had already taken photos of Chairman Mao paying visit to the Soviet Union and working at the construction site of the Ming Tombs Reservoir Project. His portfolio also includes other prominent names among China's first generation of leaders, such as Zhou Enlai, Liu Shaoqi, Deng Xiaoping. As China entered the new era of reform and opening-up, it was no surprise for Yang Shaoming to shift his attention to Deng Xiaoping, the chief architect of China's reform and opening-up. While far from being the only photographer to zoom in on Deng, Yang Shaoming's photographs of Deng Xiaoping's life and leadership are unrivaled both in length and depth. From 1962 to 1992, Yang Shaoming took numerous photos of Deng Xiaoping. The themes of the photos range from the portrayal of Deng as a visionary and virtuous statesman to the depiction of him as an amiable and down-to-earth leader, as well as the story of him as an ordinary family man. Taken together, these photos have not only captured Deng's real-life image both as an extraordinary leader and as an ordinary man from an aesthetic sense, but also provided a first-hand and touching testimony for the dramatic history of contemporary China. Through the camera of Yang Shaoming, the viewers are able to observe Deng Xiaoping's life and career, as he confronted the challenges of governing China, and steered the course of the country's reform and opening-up until his retirement. Having decided to make Deng Xiaoping the primary focus of his photography, Yang Shaoming devoted his efforts to capturing Deng's historical footsteps with his outstanding photos.

The style in which Yang Shaoming took photos of Deng Xiaoping was strikingly different from that of photographers in foreign countries. Priding himself as a disciple of Henri Cartier-Bresson (1908—2004), the French master photographer, Yang Shaoming has skillfully applied Cartier-Bresson's concept of "decisive moment" to news photography. As a result, Yang Shaoming's photography is filled with decisive moments in history, as he often chooses the right story to tell at the right time and place, adding his unique discoveries and interpretations. He is also adept at speaking in the special language of photography, revealing unspoken truths with visible images while integrating artistic intuition with philosophical thinking, so as to create a strong impact from the outside to the inside. When Deng Xiaoping began his southern tour inspecting coastal cities for their opening-up in the spring of 1992, Yang Shaoming was quick to recognize the tour's historical significance and decided to tag along. The photos he took of Deng Xiaoping mingling with the masses and exuding great confidence on the tour received immediate, overwhelming responses after being published in China's major newspapers. Seeing these meaningful photos, the Chinese people felt a liberating sense of "early spring in the South", and could envision the coming of a new "spring" in socialist China.

The ways in which Yang Shaoming took photos of Deng Xiaoping were also easily distinguishable from those of his Chinese counterparts. Breaking with tradition, he decided to approach Deng Xiaoping not as an out-of-reach and formidable leader, but simply as a kind old man who loves his country and people and wants to do good for them. By placing the great man among his people and his family, Yang Shaoming was able to show us what Deng Xiaoping was really like, both as a political leader and as an ordinary man, and such is the genius of his photography. For example, in a 1980 photo titled "In Love with His Hometown", Yang Shaoming truthfully captured the image of Deng Xiaoping as "a man of the people" who had his own sincere feelings.

Yang Shaoming's efforts to tell true stories about Deng Xiaoping were recognized when he was awarded an important prize in the 31st World Press Photo Contest for his photo series "Deng

Xiaoping in His Retirement". Because no photographer from China had ever won a WPP award before, this was truly a record-breaking achievement for Chinese photography. The award was also an important milestone in Yang Shaoming's career of news photography, not only winning him acclaim at home and abroad, but also establishing him as a leading figure in taking photos of China's leaders.

As far as Yang Shaoming is concerned, photography is a product of technological development, and today's state-of-the-art technologies provide infinite possibilities for the revolution of photography. Therefore, the only way to realize a photographer's full potential is by truly learning the skills of the trade, and he certainly practices what he preaches. He has not only mastered the art of using light and taking snapshots in photography, but also acquired the ability to turn the impossible into possible under unfavorable circumstances. With confidence and superior skills, he has captured exciting moments even in dim light, put his life on the line for some good shots, snapped numerous pictures just to get a scoop, and achieved unexpected success in the most difficult situations. All in all, Yang Shaoming's talents and virtuosity have not only assured his success as a news photographer, but also added a unique layer of personality to his artistic pursuits.

Ke Ling, a well-known Chinese writer, once made the following comments about Yang Shaoming as one of contemporary China's best photographers: "With exceptional perception, accuracy, judgment and decisiveness, the photographer travels through boundless time and space seeking his subjects. He turns fleeting moments into eternity as he presses the shutter, just like a flashlight, on the right occasion, at the right moment and from the right angle."

A true masterpiece of photography not only provides its audience with aesthetic pleasures, but also enlightens their mind and heart, if not awakens their soul. Just like one tree shaking another tree, one cloud touching another cloud, and one soul waking another soul. Just like that, Yang Shaoming took photo after photo to record our past and present, highlighting the value and magic of photography, while leaving photographic landmarks of decisive moments in China's history.

目录
Contents

风　云　人　物
AN EXTRAORDINARY LEADER

1979年1月和1986年1月，邓小平两度成为美国《时代周刊》年度风云人物

Time magazine has twice named Deng Xiaoping as its **Man of the Year**, first in January 1979 and again in January 1986

在中国共产党的历史上，邓小平占据了非常重要的地位。他意志坚强，目光远大，干练果断，以在长期革命斗争中所建立的功勋，以坚定的马克思主义者的智慧、魄力和威望，赢得了人民的信任和爱戴。

中华人民共和国成立以后，他是党的第一代中央领导集体的重要成员，是第二代领导集体的核心。他以非凡的勇气大胆纠正党在特殊年代所犯的严重错误，拨正了中国革命的船头，使中国走出动荡，走向繁荣富强。他是神州大地上空的一盏明灯，无数次驱走黑暗，点亮未来。

伟人走了，事业未竟。他将丰功伟绩留给了神州大地，他将音容笑貌铭刻在各族儿女的脑海心田。

邓小平是一位有世界眼光的国际活动家，为了给中国的改革开放创建一个十分有利的国际环境，他以充沛的精力进行外事活动，虚心学习发达国家的成功经验，大胆从资本主义国家引进资金技术，拉开了“对内改革，对外开放”的划时代的历史大幕。他频繁接见外国来宾，出访许多发达国家，接触外国政要、著名企业家和各界知名人士，呕心沥血地为中国改革开放谋篇布局，大刀阔斧地开展外交活动，把世界的目光吸引到中国来，为中国的经济发展赢得了宝贵机遇和时间，也深刻影响了世界历史的进程。1979年1月、1986年1月，他两度成为美国《时代周刊》的年度风云人物。

Deng Xiaoping has certainly played an essential role in the history of the Communist Party of China (CPC). He has transformed modern China with his determination, vision and effective leadership. He has won enormous trust and respect from the Chinese people for his revolutionary accomplishments, and for his wisdom and prestige as a true Marxist.

Since the founding of the People's Republic of China, Deng Xiaoping has been a key member of the first generation of CPC leaders, and he is the core of the second generation of CPC leaders. With extraordinary courage and leadership, he corrected the mistakes of the Cultural Revolution and brought the country back to order and normalcy. The various reform programs that he had initiated eventually launched China on a path of phenomenal economic growth and prosperity. Like a bright lamp hanging over China, he had guided the Chinese people out of darkness and lighted up their future countless times.

The death of Deng Xiaoping is far from the end of his great cause. His enduring accomplishments will forever be remembered by his motherland, and he will always be alive in the hearts of the Chinese people.

Deng Xiaoping was an extraordinary international activist with a global vision. In order to create a favorable international environment for China's reform and opening-up, he had committed himself to diplomatic activities with abundant energy, and initiated the historic reform and opening-up of China. He was humble and open-minded when he learned successful experience from developed countries, and he was audacious when he imported foreign investment and technology from capitalist countries. He met with foreign guests frequently, visited numerous developed countries, and made friends with global leaders, famous entrepreneurs and celebrities from all walks of life. He designed China's reform and opening-up program with painstaking efforts, and pushed through China's diplomatic campaign to connect with the world. Through his tireless efforts, he had earned time and precious opportunities for the country's economic development. The fact that he had been twice named Man of the Year by *Time* magazine testifies to his profound influence on the course of human history.

大阅兵

1984 年 10 月 1 日，为庆祝中华人民共和国成立 35 周年，国庆阅兵在北京天安门广场隆重举行。这是中华人民共和国成立后的第 12 次大阅兵，亦是继 1959 年国庆后首次盛大的国庆阅兵，具有非同寻常的意义。担任这次检阅的阅兵首长的，正是中国改革开放的总设计师邓小平。身着中山装的邓小平，站在设有扶手的检阅车上，检阅了中国人民解放军受阅部队，他对国家的前途命运充满信心，那种精神和气魄，令国内外观众终生难忘。

The Grand Military Parade

On October 1, 1984, a grand military parade was held at Tiananmen Square in Beijing to mark the 35th anniversary of the founding of the People's Republic of China. This was the 12th grand military parade held since the founding of the PRC, as well as the first one to be held on National Day since 1959. The chief inspector of this truly significant parade was none other than Deng Xiaoping, the chief architect of China's reform and opening up. Deng wore a Mao suit and stood in the sunroof of a Red Flag limousine with special rails. As he inspected the People's Liberation Army troops, he had truly impressed audiences at home and abroad with his high spirits and great confidence in China's future.

中央军委主席邓小平乘敞篷车，出天安门，过金水桥，检阅中国人民解放军受阅部队。

This photo was taken at the moment when Deng Xiaoping, then Chairman of the Central Military Commission, stood in the sunroof of a limousine and started his inspection of the PLA troops, just as he was leaving Tiananmen Rostrum through the famous Jinshui Bridge.

民共和国万岁
A01-3430

拍“办公照”

1984 年夏天，我受新华社领导委托，要在北戴河为小平同志拍摄“工作照”。卓琳阿姨很高兴，让家里的孩子们帮我把摄影器材扛到小平同志的办公室里。我表达了请求后，不料小平同志张口就一句：“我从来就不办公！拍什么工作照？”一时间大家全愣住了。卓琳阿姨连忙打圆场，我很快领会了邓伯伯的意思，他讨厌搞形式主义。他处理文件，通常是在起居室里，而不是在办公室。尴尬之际，老人家还是给了我一个台阶下：“只此一次，下不为例。”

Taking Photos of Deng Xiaoping “Working in the Office”

In the summer of 1984, I was assigned a task by Xinhua News Agency to take some “work photos” of Deng Xiaoping in Beidaihe. Aunt Zhuo Lin, Deng’s wife, was cheerful about it and asked her children to help me carry the equipment to Deng’s office. To everyone’s surprise, Deng turned down my request by saying,“I never work in the office! What work photos?” For a while, everyone was stunned. While Aunt Zhuo Lin quickly saved us from embarrassment, I began to understand why Uncle Deng raised his objections. He was saying NO to formalism. It was usually in his living room where he dealt with the paperwork, not in the office. To save me from further embarrassment, Uncle Deng fulfilled my request for a photo, adding,“This is a one-time deal.”

9:14

邓小平在北京中南海紫光阁接受美国哥伦比亚广播公司（CBS）《60 分钟》电视新闻访谈节目主持人迈克·华莱士的专访。
Deng Xiaoping took an interview with CBS's *"60 Minutes"* correspondent Mike Wallace in the Ziguang Pavilion of Zhongnanhai.

重要谈话

1986 年 9 月 2 日，邓小平在北京中南海紫光阁接受美国哥伦比亚广播公司（CBS）《60 分钟》电视新闻访谈节目主持人迈克·华莱士（Mike Wallace，1918—2012）的专访。邓小平作为出色的国际战略家和杰出的外交家，从容不迫地回答了华莱士提出的各种问题，包括中苏关系、中美关系、台湾问题、中国的经济和政治改革以及干部退休制度等。

华莱士问道："邓小平以后的中国会怎样？是否会回到过去的状况？"邓小平回答："肯定不会。"邓小平坚定实行改革开放的声音，通过华莱士传播到全世界，让世界对开放的中国有了一个清楚的了解。

一个小时后，礼宾司宣布采访到此结束，小平同志按着扶手正准备站起来，华莱士却横生枝节，执意要再追加一个问题："您什么时候退下来？"小平同志很耐心地倾听了他的问题，然后毫不掩饰地说："我坦率地告诉你，我正在说服人们，到明年党的十三大时就退下来，但到今天为止，我听到的是一片反对之声。"

华莱士对邓小平的访谈时间比原定的一个小时增加了 20 分钟。采访结束时，华莱士走到邓小平面前，对自己的失礼表示歉意。邓小平并不介意，友好地与其握手道别。

这次采访让华莱士毕生难忘，他真实感受到了邓小平为人坦率、和蔼可亲、平易近人的一面。华莱士回忆采访邓小平时说道："我见过很多世界领导人，邓小平和别人不一样，他是独一无二的。"

An Important Interview with Mike Wallace

On September 2, 1986, Deng Xiaoping took an interview with CBS's *"60 Minutes"* correspondent Mike Wallace (1918-2012) in the Ziguang Pavilion of Zhongnanhai. During the interview, Deng Xiaoping demonstrated his outstanding strategic thinking and diplomatic skills, as he calmly explained China's economic and political policies and clarified its position on various important issues, including Sino-Soviet relations, Sino-US relations and the Taiwan issue as well as the institution of a retirement system for Chinese leaders.

During the interview, Wallace asked: "What would happen to China after Deng Xiaoping is gone? Would things go back to the way they were before?" Deng Xiaoping gave a firm answer, "Certainly there will be no turning back." The Chinese leader's resolute commitment to the country's reform and opening-up was heard loud and clear around the world, while the world had gained a better understanding of where China was going from this interview.

As the interview was scheduled to end after one hour, Wallace insisted on adding one last question for Deng Xiaoping, who was ready to stand up by pressing the handrail of his chair. "How long do you intend to continue to be the chief leader and the chief adviser?" Wallace asked. After hearing Wallace out, Deng Xiaoping gave him an honest answer, "To be quite frank, I am trying to persuade people to let me retire at the Party's 13th National Congress next year. But so far, all I have heard is dissenting voices on all sides." At the end of the interview, which lasted 20 minutes longer than originally scheduled, Wallace walked up to Deng Xiaoping and apologized for causing him the inconvenience. Deng did not mind at all, as he shook hands with Wallace and said goodbye in a friendly manner.

The interview proved unforgettable for Wallace who felt Deng was a person who was frank, amiable and easy to approach, "I met many world leaders, Deng is different from the others, he is unique", this is how Wallace recalled the interview.

邓小平与迈克·华莱士握手。

Deng Xiaoping shaking hands with Mike Wallace.

正负电子对撞机奠基仪式

1984 年 10 月 7 日，中国正负电子对撞机国家实验室在北京西郊奠基。上午，邓小平参加了奠基典礼。刚一下汽车，邓小平就握住了美籍华裔物理学家李政道的手，说："应该感谢你的关心和支持，希望你继续帮助建造北京正负电子对撞机。" 1988 年 10 月 16 日，中国第一座高能加速器——北京正负电子对撞机首次对撞成功，成为我国继原子弹、氢弹爆炸成功、人造卫星上天后，在高科技领域的又一重大突破性成就，奠定了我国在国际高能物理界的地位。1988 年 10 月 24 日，邓小平在正负电子对撞机建成典礼上说："过去也好，今天也好，未来也好，中国必须发展自己的高科技，在世界高科技领域占有一席之地。"

Laying the Foundation Stone for China's First Electron-Positron Collider

On October 7, 1984, the groundbreaking ceremony was held for the first Chinese Electron-Positron Collider in the west suburb of Beijing, with Deng Xiaoping and other top Chinese leaders participating. As soon as he got off the car, Deng Xiaoping shook hands with the famous Chinese-American physicist Tsung-Dao Lee and said, "I must thank you for your participation and support. I hope you will continue to help us build the Electron-Positron Collider." On October 16, 1988, China's first electron-positron collisions took place at the Beijing Electron-Positron Collider. Following the successful explosion of atomic and hydrogen bombs as well as the launching of satellites, this was yet another major breakthrough for China in its development of high technology, which truly established the country's position in the international community of high-energy physics. On October 24,1988, when Deng Xiaoping came back once more to the site where four years ago he had laid the foundation stone, he delivered an important speech, declaring that, "It has always been, and will always be, necessary for China to develop its own high technology so that it can take its place in this field."

邓小平与美籍华裔物理学家李政道（左一）亲切握手。（左三为杨尚昆，左四为李鹏，右一为周光召）

Deng Xiaoping warmly shaking hands with Chinese-American physicist Tsung-Dao Lee (first from left). (third from left, Yang Shangkun; fourth from left, Li Peng; first from right, Zhou Guangzhao)

邓小平和哈默博士

邓小平在对外开放的策略中，最具有创新和突破意义的就是利用外资。1987 年 9 月 13 日，邓小平会见美国西方石油公司董事长阿曼德·哈默（Armand Hammer，1898—1990）。邓小平强调，中国要发展，离开改革开放是不可能的，今后我们要更加开放，还要加快改革的步子。89 岁的哈默博士八次访问中国，多次受到邓小平的接见。两位老朋友再次见面，彼此热情地握手、拥抱，祝贺中国同西方石油公司的合作取得重大成果。

Deng Xiaoping and His Old Friend Armand Hammer

The most innovative strategy in Deng Xiaoping's opening-up campaign was the use of foreign investments. On September 13, 1987, Deng Xiaoping met with his old friend Armand Hammer (1898-1990), who was chairman of the Occidental Petroleum Corporation. At the meeting, Deng Xiaoping stressed the importance for China to carry on its reform and opening-up, while doing so at much greater pace. The 89-year-old Dr. Hammer had visited China eight times, and was received by Deng Xiaoping on several occasions. When the two old friends met once again, they shook hands and hugged each other, sharing their joy on the significant achievements from the cooperation between China and Occidental Petroleum.

邓小平与美国大通·曼哈顿银行国际咨询委员会代表团合影。（前排左一为荣毅仁，左二为大卫·洛克菲勒，右一为基辛格）

Deng Xiaoping taking a photo with the delegation of the International Advisory Board of Chase Manhattan Bank. (front row, first from left, Rong Yiren; second from left, David Rockefeller; first from right, Henry Kissinger)

接见美国大通·曼哈顿银行国际咨询委员会代表团

1988 年 5 月 24 日，邓小平在北京人民大会堂会见美国大通·曼哈顿银行国际咨询委员会代表团。这个代表团是来北京出席该银行举行的国际咨询委员会会议的，代表团成员来自 15 个国家。会谈结束后集体合影时，邓小平与基辛格博士等人热情握手。邓小平多次提出要大胆利用外资。要引进外资，就必须为外商创造比较好的条件。邓小平指出：“要人家来投资，不让人家赚钱是不行的。有些费用太高，人家就赚不了钱。这方面我们要下决心解决。”引进国外人才，利用国外智力资源，正是邓小平的又一重要设想。

Meeting with the Delegation of the International Advisory Board of Chase Manhattan Bank

Deng Xiaoping met with the Delegation of the International Advisory Board of Chase Manhattan Bank in the Great Hall of the People in Beijing on May 24, 1988. The delegation, which came to Beijing to attend Chase's International Advisory Board meeting, was composed of delegates from 15 countries. During the group photo session after the meeting, Deng Xiaoping warmly shook hands with Dr. Henry Kissinger and other delegates. Deng Xiaoping had repeatedly stressed the importance of taking advantage of foreign investment, as well as the need to create better conditions for foreign investors. As he pointed out: "You just have to find ways to let the foreign investors make money. If the cost is too high, no one makes money. This is the problem we have to solve with great determination." It was indeed one of Deng Xiaoping's great ideas to attract foreign talents and tap into foreign intellectual resources.

邓小平应邀出席兆龙饭店举行的开业剪彩仪式。（左一为包玉刚，后中为习仲勋，右一为万里）

Deng Xiaoping attending the ribbon-cutting ceremony for the grand opening of Zhaolong Hotel. (first from left, Yue-Kong Pao; middle in the back, Xi Zhongxun; first from right, Wan Li)

兆龙饭店开业

有“世界船王”美誉的香港实业家包玉刚，积极拓展国际海运事业，支持和内地旅游部门合资建设旅游设施。他和国家旅游局合作，在北京捐资修建以自己父亲包兆龙的名字命名的“兆龙饭店”。1985 年 10 月，由邓小平亲笔题写店名的兆龙饭店落成，邓小平应邀出席开业剪彩仪式，给了包玉刚特殊的礼遇。

The Grand Opening of Zhaolong Hotel

Yue-Kong Pao, nicknamed “King of the Sea” and the founder of Hong Kong’s Worldwide Shipping Group, was noted not only for his success as an international shipping magnate, but also for his enthusiastic support for and investment in the development of the Chinese mainland’s tourism industry. With China’s National Tourism Administration as partner, he donated and built the Zhaolong Hotel in Beijing, which was named after his father Bao Zhaolong. In recognition of Yue-Kong Pao’s great contribution to China’s tourism development, Deng Xiaoping himself inscribed the name for the hotel and attended its grand opening in October 1985.

第一次公开言退

邓小平同志无论是对党内，还是对外国新闻记者，都明确而清晰地表明在干部问题上“废除终身制，建立退休制”的一贯主张。经历了相当长的一段时间之后，他老人家富于远见卓识的主张才终于得以实现。

1987 年 10 月 25 日，在中国共产党第十三次全国代表大会期间，邓小平佩戴出席证来到人民大会堂 118 厅。他在与老同志见面时发表了即兴讲话，明确提出“这一届一批老同志要退下来”的主张。

邓小平“言退”一言既出，当时在会的老一辈无产阶级革命家，包括周恩来总理的夫人邓颖超、当年同邓小平一起留法勤工俭学的聂荣臻元帅，都一致表示支持和拥护。邓小平走到他们身边，与他们一一握手，以表达谢意。

邓小平与聂荣臻元帅（右）亲切握手。（左一为邓颖超）

Deng Xiaoping cordially shaking hands with Marshal Nie Rongzhen (right). (first from left, Deng Yingchao)

Deng Xiaoping's First Public Announcement of Retirement

Whether he was speaking to comrades within the CPC or to foreign correspondents, Deng Xiaoping had always taken a clear and consistent position on the issue of abolishing the system of life tenure in leading posts and establishing a system of retirement. It actually took a long while before his visionary ideas in this regard had been put into practice.

On October 25, 1987, during the 13th National Congress of the CPC, Deng Xiaoping delivered an impromptu speech when meeting with his old comrades in the Great Hall of the People, where he explicitly put forward the idea that,"A group of old comrades have to retire from their posts after this conference."

Once Deng Xiaoping made clear his intentions on the issue of retirement, the seasoned proletarian revolutionaries who were present, including Deng Yingchao, wife of Premier Zhou Enlai, and Marshal Nie Rongzhen, who work-studied in France with Deng Xiaoping, all unanimously expressed their support and approval for Deng's proposal. In order to express his appreciation for their support, Deng Xiaoping walked up to his old comrades and shook hands with them one by one.

竹下登访华

日本首相竹下登（Takeshita Noboru，1924—2000）自 1972 年以来曾四次访问中国。他多年来重视发展日中友好关系，并为此做出了重要贡献。1988 年 8 月 25 日，竹下登访华，承诺向中国提供第三批政府贷款。1988 年 8 月 26 日，邓小平会见了来访的竹下登首相，他说："我昨天晚上特意从北戴河回来欢迎你。希望我们之间能够建立起不低于田中、大平时代的新关系。我讲田中、大平时代的关系，主要指相互信任。发展两国关系，要建立在相互信任的基础上。"

Takeshita Noboru, the Prime Minister of Japan, Paying a Visit to China

Takeshita Noboru (1924-2000), who served as the Prime Minister of Japan from 1987 to 1989, had visited China four times since 1972. He had always attached great importance to developing friendly relations between Japan and China, and had made important contributions toward this end. During his trip to China on August 25, 1988, Prime Minister Takeshita pledged the third batch of the Japanese government's loans to China. Deng Xiaoping met with Takeshita on August 26, 1988, and made the following comments about China-Japan relations: "I made some special arrangements to come back from Beidaihe last night just for our meeting today. It is my hope that China and Japan can forge a new relationship that is as good as, if not better than, the one we had during the Tanaka and Ohira eras, especially in terms of building mutual trust. The strengthening of bilateral ties depends on our mutual trust."

大国博弈

乔治·赫伯特·沃克·布什（George Herbert Walker Bush，1924—2018）在 1974 年至 1975 年间曾担任美国驻华联络处主任，后于 1989 年至 1993 年出任美国第 41 任总统，他对邓小平的改革开放给中国带来的变化有切身的体会。1989 年 2 月 26 日，邓小平在北京人民大会堂接见布什总统。按以往惯例，新当选的美国总统出访的第一站，基本都是选择西欧盟国，而这次布什却打破常规，借出席日本天皇裕仁的葬礼之机提前访问了中国，证明了中国在他心目中的重要地位。

Great Power Politics

Before becoming the 41st president of the United States from 1989 to 1993, George Herbert Walker Bush (1924-2018) served as Chief of the U.S. Liaison Office in the People's Republic of China from 1974 to 1975. Acting as the de facto American ambassador to China, he gained firsthand experience of the profound changes that China's reform and opening-up had brought to the country. On February 26, 1989, Deng Xiaoping met with President Bush at the Great Hall of the People in Beijing. Traditionally, the newly elected American president would make one of its European allies the destination of his or her first presidential trip aboard. However, the fact that President Bush broke the norm and visited China after attending the funeral of Japanese Emperor Hirohito speaks volumes about China's rising status in the American president's mind.

迎接金日成

1989年11月5日，朝鲜劳动党中央委员会总书记金日成应邀来华访问，邓小平率新一届领导班子到北京火车站迎接。中朝两国向来是友好邻邦，多年的患难与共也让两国领导人结下了深情厚谊。金日成看到85岁高龄的邓小平还亲自到车站迎接他，十分感动，快步上前，和邓小平紧紧拥抱。邓小平在车站告诉金日成："我已向中共中央政治局提出辞去党和国家军委主席的职务。"

Greeting Kim Il-sung at the Beijing Railway Station

On November 5, 1989, Kim Il-Sung, the then General Secretary of the Central Committee of the Workers' Party of Korea, visited China upon invitation. On his arrival at the Beijing Railway Station, Kim was warmly greeted by Deng Xiaoping, along with the newly elected leadership of China. China and the Democratic People's Republic of Korea have always been friendly neighbors, and strong ties have been forged between leaders of the two countries through years of mutual support. Kim was truly moved when Deng Xiaoping, 85 years old at the time, met him in person at the station. As the two leaders hugged each other affectionately, Deng Xiaoping informed Kim that he had submitted his resignation, to the Political Bureau of the CPC Central Committee, of his post of Chairman of the Central Military Commission.

大地之子

1979 年，经邓小平提议，五届全国人大六次会议批准，把 3 月 12 日定为“中国植树节”。这个决议为中国的植树造林事业带来了春天。在北京中央机关的植树点，每年的 3 月 12 日，邓小平都会率领中央领导同志和中直机关的干部到这里参加植树劳动。这是 1983 年植树节，邓小平和中央领导同志一起参加植树劳动的情景。抓住邓小平直起腰身、接受新华社记者专访的宝贵时机，我伏下身子，采用大仰角，运用低侧光，借助远近视差构图技巧，拍下了这位矗立于天地之间、充满自信的伟人的瞬间。

Son of the Earth

By the suggestion of Deng Xiaoping, March 12 had been officially designated as China's National Tree Planting Day at the 6th Session of the 5th National People's Congress. The establishment of a national Arbor Day literally brought the country's forests back to life. Every year on March 12, Deng Xiaoping would attend tree planting activities with other leaders of the CPC Central Committee at the tree planting site of the central government in Beijing. This photo was taken on the Arbor Day of 1983, when Deng Xiaoping was participating in a tree planting activity as usual. Just as Deng Xiaoping straightened up for an interview with Xinhua News Agency, I crouched down and captured the moment when he stood up with pride and confidence as China's great leader. In this photo, I shot at a low angle and used side light, and applied the technique of near-far composition.

喜摘咖啡豆

1960 年 1 月 31 日，邓小平于腿伤康复期间到海南岛视察工作。在兴隆华侨农场，小平一行先后参观了咖啡园、胡椒园、可可园和热带植物园。

这次的海南之行，邓小平对海南岛优越的地理环境和独特的热带自然资源印象十分深刻，强调要把海南岛好好地开发起来，将其建设成为我国重要的热带作物基地。这成为后来他倡议开发海南岛、设立海南经济特区的历史渊源。

Harvesting Coffee Beans

On January 31, 1960, Deng Xiaoping went on an inspection tour to Hainan Island as he was recuperating from a leg injury. At the Xinglong Overseas Chinese Farm, Deng Xiaoping visited the gardens where coffee pepper and cocoa were planted as well as the tropical botanical garden.

The trip to Hainan had left Deng Xiaoping with a deep impression about the island's superior geographic environment and unique tropical natural resources. Even back then, he had stressed the importance of developing Hainan in a suitable manner, so as to build it into one of the country's core tropical crop bases. This had become the historical origins of his initiative to develop Hainan Island and establish the Hainan Special Economic Zone.

图为小平同志在兴隆华侨农场采摘咖啡豆的生动画面，是我青年时期的作品，也是小平同志当年视察海南岛期间为数不多的珍贵历史镜头。

This photo was taken when Deng Xiaoping was harvesting coffee beans at the Xinglong Overseas Chinese Farm. It was one of my early works as well as one of the few precious historical pictures of Deng Xiaoping during his 1960 visit to Hainan Island.

植树节

1983 年植树节，邓小平和胡耀邦、习仲勋等中央领导同志来到北京中央机关植树基地，参加植树劳动。在国家领导人的倡导下，植树节成为全民参与的重大节日。

植树节从正式设立至今已 40 多载，祖国的万里山河也发生了巨变，当年的树苗已经长成参天大树，郁郁葱葱的森林为共和国的大地披上了新装。林业不仅为国家提供了丰厚的资源，还有效地维护了国土生态安全。

Tree Planting on Arbor Day

On the National Tree Planting Day of 1983, Deng Xiaoping, along with Hu Yaobang, Xi Zhongxun and other leaders of the CPC Central Committee, participated in the annual tree planting activity in Beijing. Deng Xiaoping and other Chinese leaders have led the efforts to plant trees and promote a harmonious relationship between humans and nature.

It has been more than 40 years since the official establishment of China's Arbor Day, and the magnificent landscape of China has undergone great changes since then. The saplings planted by the elder generation have now grown into towering trees, while the lush forests have painted the country green. China's forest industry has not only provided the country with abundant resources, but also safeguarded the national ecological security.

参加植树劳动。（后左一为习仲勋，后左二为姚依林，右一为胡耀邦）

Planting trees on Arbor Day. (first from left in the back, Xi Zhongxun; second from left in the back, Yao Yilin; first from right, Hu Yaobang)

登峨眉

1980 年夏，我碰巧在成都遇到了小平同志，第二天就跟着他老人家一起爬了峨眉山，有幸抓拍到了这张《乡情》，也是领袖在人民群众中富有人情味的一个经典画面。小平同志曾经说过：“我是中国人民的儿子，我深情地爱着我的祖国和人民。”“与人民在一起，是我最高兴的事情。”我抓拍的正是这个时代的一个伟大主题。

Hiking up Mount Emei

In the summer of 1980, I happened to come across Deng Xiaoping in Chengdu, and went with him the next day for a hiking tour of Mount Emei. During the trip, I was lucky to capture this enduring moment, when Deng Xiaoping revealed an unusual side as a great leader who was also deeply attached to the ordinary people. Deng Xiaoping used to say, "I am the son of the Chinese people, and I love my motherland and people deeply." "It gives me the greatest pleasure when I am with the ordinary people." The moment that I had captured in this photo was a true manifestation of the greatness of Deng Xiaoping.

路遇“老庚”的老大娘

那天，小平同志穿着汗衫，挽起裤腿，手拄竹杖，一路上和我们谈笑风生。途中，遇见一位老大娘。在我远远地看到这位老大娘时，马上产生一种预判，一旦小平同志与她攀谈，肯定会出现一个极好的拍摄机会。于是我加快脚步，赶到了队伍的最前边。

果然，小平同志亲切地问老大娘：“老乡，离万年寺还有多远？”老大娘没有想到眼前的这位老人就是邓小平，听到问话，漫不经心地回答：“不远喽，就在前面。”小平同志一听很高兴，连忙说：“好，我们加快点儿。”

等我们快到万年寺的时候，发现这位老大娘紧追不舍地赶上来了。她追上小平同志，不容分说，就要下跪，她要感谢小平同志。小平同志看了看老大娘，又看了看我们周围的人，说：“又不是要拜菩萨。”大家一阵开怀大笑。

小平同志边说边把老大娘扶起来，问：“老人家，多大年纪了？”她说：“76 岁了。”小平同志说：“啊呀，我们两个是老庚呐！”这个“老庚”，在我们四川话里就是同年的意思。

小平同志问她：“现在生活如何？”这位老大娘说：“啊呀，比过去我们农村不晓得好到哪里去了！”

An Interesting Encounter on Mount Emei

Wearing a white short-sleeve shirt that day, Deng Xiaoping was in great spirits when he climbed Mount Emei. Pulling his trousers up and walking with a bamboo stick, Deng talked and smiled along the trip. On the way to Wannian Temple, we met with an old lady who was sitting on a rock and resting. When I saw her from afar, I had the feeling that it would make a great photo if Deng Xiaoping should strike up a conversation with her. Without much thinking, I rushed to the front of the entourage.

Just as I had predicted, Deng Xiaoping kindly asked the old lady, “Lao Xiang (Sichuanese, meaning people who share the same hometown), how far is it from here to Wannian Temple?” Not knowing the true identity of Deng Xiaoping at the time, the old lady answered casually, “Not too far, it’s just ahead.” Deng was really glad to hear this, as he told everyone, “Great, let’s pick up the pace.”

Just as we were about to reach Wannian Temple, the old lady had caught up with us, having learned about Deng’s true identity. The moment she saw Deng Xiaoping, she almost knelt down and said her thanks to him. At this point, Deng jokingly said, “It’s not like you’re worshipping the Buddha.” This remark got everyone laughing.

As he hurriedly helped the old lady up, Deng Xiaoping asked her, “How old are you, old lady?” She replied, “I’m already 76 years old.” Upon hearing this, Deng said, “Well, that makes us a pair of Lao Geng!” In Sichuanese, the word “Lao Geng” refers to people who were born in the same year.

Deng Xiaoping continued to ask her, “How’s life nowadays?” The old lady happily replied, “Life nowadays is so much better than the past, even for the countryside!”

拨浪

8 月的北戴河海滨，碧空如洗，阳光给海湾镀上了一层金色。

在几名年轻水手的护卫下，邓小平踏浪下海。他稳健地走在最前边，熟练地展开双臂，在海面上拨起层层浪花。小平同志说过："在大自然中游泳，自由度大一些，有股气势。"

我早已端着相机先小平同志一步闯进水中。看到小平拨起的浪花在阳光的照耀下闪烁，很是灵动，在天水之间增添了无限生气，构成了一幅动静相宜的美妙画面，我兴奋极了。为了凸显小平同志的主体形象，我极力压低拍摄角度，举着双镜头相机，仰着脖子观看取景框。小平同志在水中走得很快，我也不得不连连后退，不料退到深水处，海水马上就要没到嘴巴里了。我相信自己的水性，愣是咬牙坚持着，等到主人公情绪最饱满的刹那，果断按下了快门。

Playing with the Waves

Under the clear blue sky, the sun gilded a golden layer on the Beidaihe beach in August.

Guarded by several young men behind him, Deng Xiaoping calmly stepped into the sea and skillfully played with the waves. He used to say, "A person enjoys much greater freedom and power when swimming in the natural sea."

I had been waiting in the water for Deng Xiaoping with my camera ready. I was excited to see him playing with the waves in the sunlight, full of life and energy and forming a wonderful picture combining movement and stillness. In order to highlight his image, I tried my best to lower the angle, while holding up the dual-lens camera and sticking my neck above water to see the viewfinder. As Deng walked very fast in the water, I had to back up further and deeper into the sea. Not deterred by the risk of getting drowned, I gritted my teeth and held on to my camera for the perfect moment. When that moment finally came, I did not hesitate to press the shutter and captured Deng Xiaoping's image as a great man expressing his true emotions in the sea.

游泳

“我检测自己的身体靠两条：一条是能不能下海，一条是能不能打桥牌。能打桥牌证明脑袋还好，能下海证明体力还好。”（《邓小平自述》）

邓小平一生与大海结缘，酷爱在大海里游泳。他少年时远渡重洋，走上革命道路；去世后，家人遵照老人家的遗愿，将他的骨灰撒入大海，回归自然。

这位在政治风浪中泰然处之的伟人，在大海的波涛里同样是劈波斩浪，如履平地。邓小平每次在北戴河游泳，总是沿着泳区的最大边缘游，一游就是一个小时以上。1992 年，邓小平又一次来到北戴河游泳，第一次下海就游了 45 分钟。这次疗养，他总共下海 8 次，这一年他 88 岁。

Swimming in the Sea

“I have two ways to check if I am in good health or not: first, to see if I can still go swimming in the sea; second, to see if I can still play bridge. If I can play bridge, it means my mind still works; if I can swim in the sea, it means my body is healthy.” ——Quoted from *Deng Xiaoping: A Life Told in His Own Words*

Throughout his life, Deng Xiaoping has had a lasting relationship with the sea, and swimming in it was one of his biggest hobbies. When he was a young boy, he crossed the world’s oceans to begin his revolutionary life; when he passed away, his family followed his wish and scattered his ashes into the sea, returning him to nature.

As a great man who had survived and thrived through numerous “political waves”, Deng Xiaoping would always find himself at ease with the sea. He always swam close to the edge of the swimming area in Beidaihe, and he would swim for more than an hour each time. When he stayed in Beidaihe in 1992, he went swimming in the sea for a total of eight times, and he swam for 45 minutes the first time. He had already turned 88 that year.

指 点 迷 津

ARCHITECT OF MODERN CHINA

“发展才是硬道理”

“Development is of overriding importance”

党的十一届三中全会以后，邓小平坚定地肩负起中国改革开放的重担。改革的道路上充满荆棘，刚刚建立起来的几个经济特区虽然取得了很大成绩，可深受极左思潮影响的人，仍然把特区说得一团漆黑，深圳、珠海等经济特区承受着空前的压力。

为了护住改革开放的旗帜不被歪风吹倒，1984 年春，邓小平首次去南方视察，实地考察特区的真实情况。几个特区在短短几年内取得的辉煌成就，更加坚定了邓小平推行改革开放的信心。他挥笔写下了“珠海经济特区好”“深圳的发展和经验证明，我们建立经济特区的政策是正确的”“把经济特区办得更快些更好些”的光辉题词，不仅为身陷重围的特区解了围，也为全国的改革开放事业注入了强大动力。

20 世纪 90 年代初，国际形势动荡，国内的一些人又开始向改革开放发难，一度掀起了姓“社”还是姓“资”的争议，把经济特区视为“疫区”，再加之党内形式主义、官僚主义盛行，改革开放事业面临严峻挑战。在这紧要关头，88 岁的邓小平在 1992 年春又踏上了去南方视察之路。一路上，针对国内形势，他发表了许多重要讲话，严厉批评了以“左”为代表的错误倾向，指出：“谁要改变三中全会的路线、方针、政策，老百姓不答应，谁就会被打倒！”邓小平的话也代表了老百姓的心声。南方谈话公开发表后，一扫中国改革开放中的羁绊和阴霾，极大地解放了人们的思想，使中国的改革开放进入了一个新的里程。

邓小平两次去南方视察，形成了威力巨大的“冲击波”，他以非凡的魄力扭转了乾坤。

Deng Xiaoping had assumed responsibility for leading China on the path of reform and opening-up since the 3rd Plenary Session of the 11th Central Committee. Reform was always full of challenges. Those who were still being affected by the "Left" tendencies had launched a smear campaign against the newly established Special Economic Zones (SEZs). Despite their impressive achievements, Shenzhen, Zhuhai and other SEZs faced unprecedented pressure at the time.

To make sure that the reform and opening-up would continue despite unfounded attacks, Deng Xiaoping embarked on his first southern tour in the spring of 1984. When he saw the SEZs' success and accomplishments with his own eyes, his faith in China's reform and opening-up was greatly reinforced. "The Zhuhai Special Economic Zone has been a success." "The development and experience of Shenzhen have proved the correctness of our policy on the establishment of Special Economic Zones." "We shall develop the Special Economic Zones in a faster and better way." As Deng Xiaoping wrote these inscriptions for the world to see, he not only relieved the SEZs of their burden and concerns, but also provided a strong impetus for the continuation of China's reform and opening-up.

China's reform and opening-up encountered yet another round of attacks amid the international turbulence in the early 1990s, as the development of the Special Economic Zones became overshadowed by a controversial debate about whether the SEZs were "socialist" or "capitalist". The upsurge of formalism and bureaucratism within the CPC also added insult to injury for the reform program. At this critical juncture, the 88-year-old Deng Xiaoping began his second southern tour in the spring of 1992. During the historic trip, he made a series of remarks that changed the course of Chinese history. He made it clear that the "Left" tendencies were more likely to ruin the country, adding that, "Anyone who attempted to change the line, principles and policies adopted since the 3rd Plenary Session of the 11th Central Committee would not be countenanced by the people; he would be toppled!" The words of Deng Xiaoping spoke the mind of ordinary Chinese. Once made public, Deng's southern talks cleared the obstacles for China's reform program in a decisive manner, liberating people's mind while revitalizing the second phase of reform and opening-up.

Deng Xiaoping's two historic southern tours would become his enduring legacy, as he had transformed modern China once again with his great vision and extraordinary leadership.

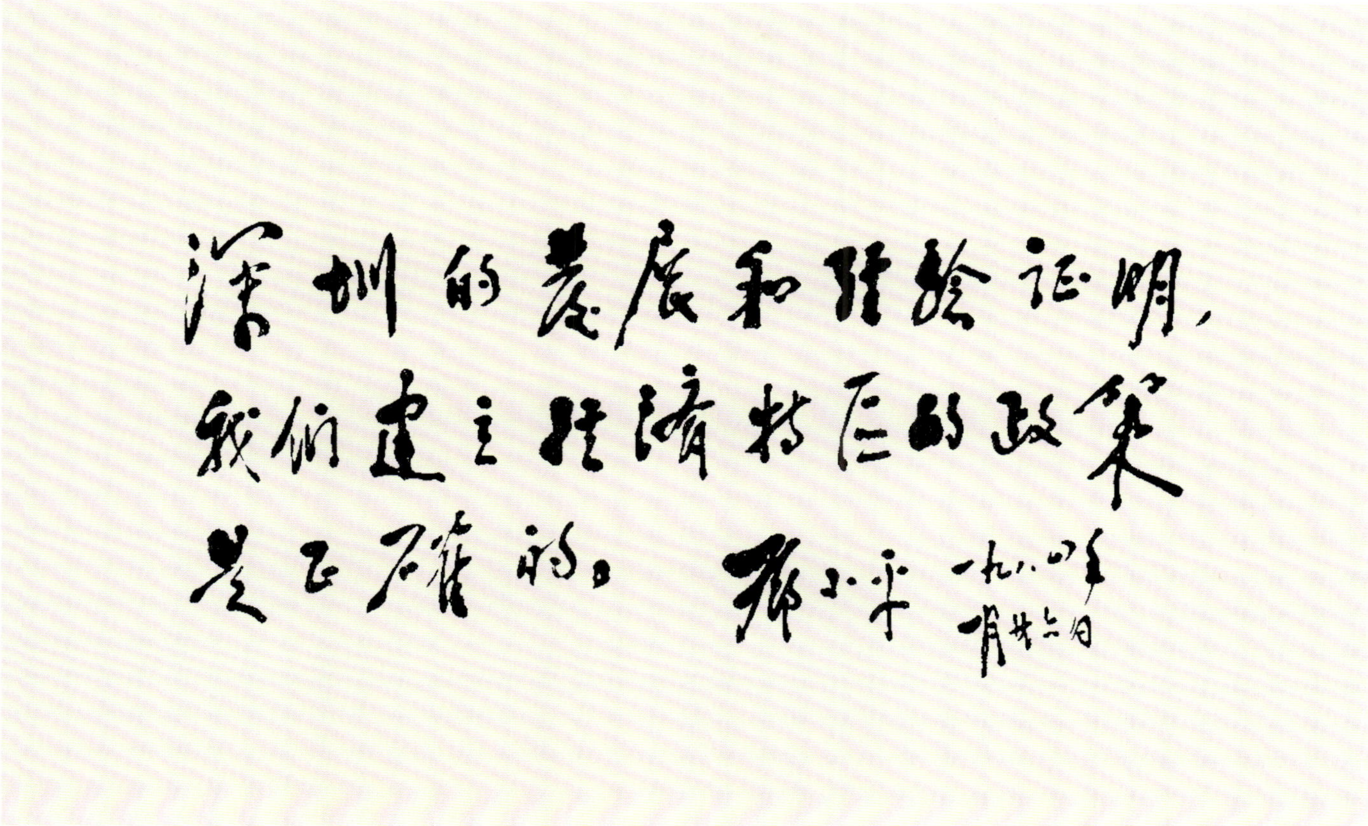

深圳的发展和经验证明，
我们建立经济特区的政策
是正确的。 邓小平 一九八四年
一月廿六日

邓小平为深圳特区题写历史性题词

结束了对深圳、珠海的视察，邓小平于 1984 年 1 月 29 日下午抵达广州，下榻在珠岛宾馆。

令深圳领导干部感到不安和不解的是：小平同志在深圳期间，既没有发表讲话，也没有为深圳题词。对于一直顶着保守势力压力的深圳来说，此时是多么渴望得到总设计师的宝贵题词。

深圳是中国第一批四个经济特区中规模最大、发展最快、成就最显著的特区。如何评价深圳，不仅是对深圳本身的简单肯定与否定，更直接关乎全国改革开放的大业。视察完深圳之后，小平同志虽然已经胸有成竹，但也没有轻易表态，他一直在思考酝酿一个既着眼深圳，也面对全国的带有总结性和政策性的题词。他把自己经过反复推敲的题词内容写在一张纸上，默默地带在身边。这些，人们并无察觉，当然翘首以盼的深圳人也无缘得知。

忐忑不安之下，深圳特区领导派人赶到广州，设法弥补。

大年三十的早上，小平同志散步回来，看见客厅的桌子上已摆好了笔墨纸砚，当得知是深圳的同志请求题词时，他平和地问道："写个啥子呢？"深圳的同志赶忙递上已经拟好的题词稿，小平同志看了一遍，把题词稿撂在一边，拿出自己预先准备好的稿子，提起笔，一字一字地写起来，让人见字知分量："深圳的发展和经验证明，我们建立经济特区的政策是正确的。"为了理顺深圳方面干部和群众的情绪，小平同志特意在题词落款中把时间提前了 6 天，点明他写题词的时间还是在他视察深圳之时。

这就是邓小平历史性题词诞生的始末。

Deng Xiaoping Writing the Historic Inscription for the Shenzhen Special Economic Zone

After finishing his inspection tour of Shenzhen and Zhuhai, Deng Xiaoping arrived in Guangzhou on the afternoon of January 29, 1984, and stayed at the Zhudao Guest House.

While he was in Shenzhen, Deng Xiaoping didn't make any remarks, nor did he write any inscriptions. This was quite disconcerting for the local leaders and cadres, who had been under enormous pressure from the conservatives within the party. How they wished to get some encouragement from the chief architect of the country's reform program.

Given its scale and speed of development as well as its success, Shenzhen was the indisputable leader among the first four Special Economic Zones in China. Therefore, the appraisal of Shenzhen was not only about the approval of one city, but actually had more to do with the evaluation of the reform and opening-up across the country. While Deng Xiaoping had already made up his mind, he didn't want to rush to any conclusions. For a while, he had been quietly contemplating what he wanted to say, not just about Shenzhen but also about the country as a whole, and he wanted to make it conclusive and politically salient. He wanted to write an inscription for Shenzhen so his messages would be remembered. He had already put down his thoughts on a piece of paper, and carried it with him without anyone knowing. Of course, the people of Shenzhen, who were eagerly anticipating something to happen, had no way of knowing this at all.

Until the anxious leaders of Shenzhen could not wait any longer and send some people to Guangzhou for an inscription from Deng Xiaoping.

When Deng Xiaoping came back from his walk on the morning of the Lunar New Year's Eve, he learned of the request for his inscription for the people of Shenzhen. While the comrades from Shenzhen had provided a draft for Deng Xiaoping's reference, he decided to write the inscription based on the draft he had prepared by himself. "The development and experience of Shenzhen have proved the correctness of our policy on the establishment of Special Economic Zones." Deng Xiaoping's approval and support for Shenzhen and other SEZs as an integral part of China's reform program was forever inscribed in these words. Considering the feelings of the cadres and people of Shenzhen, Deng Xiaoping purposefully moved the inscription date six days ahead, in order to leave the impression that the inscription had been written during his inspection tour of Shenzhen.

This was the story behind Deng Xiaoping's historic inscription for Shenzhen.

指点迷津

1992年1月至2月，88岁的邓小平由家人陪同，视察了武昌、深圳、珠海、上海等地，发表了一系列的重要谈话。“计划经济不等于社会主义，资本主义也有计划；市场经济不等于资本主义，社会主义也有市场”便是在这次南方视察中提出的。他还提出了判断姓“资”还是姓“社”的三个“有利于”的标准，鼓励大家“看准了就大胆地试，大胆地闯”，由此掀起新一轮改革高潮。邓小平的南方谈话，科学总结了党的十一届三中全会以来的实践探索和基本经验，从理论上深刻回答了长期困扰和束缚人们思想的许多重大认识问题，是把改革开放和社会主义现代化建设推向新阶段的又一个解放思想、实事求是的宣言书。

中国的改革开放中，每到一个关键的时刻，都是邓小平指点迷津。1992 年，他又以 88 岁的高龄，为改革开放事业再一次吹响了新的进军号角。邓小平，这个名字震撼寰宇，他被许多国家领导人称为“中国改革开放的总设计师”。

每到一地，我听到小平同志总要说的一句话就是：“办特区是我倡议的，中央决定的，办得怎么样，能否成功，我要亲自看一看。”

早在 1979 年 4 月的中央工作会议期间，邓小平就对当时广东省的主要负责人习仲勋、杨尚昆等提到办特区的事。小平同志说：“还是叫特区好，陕甘宁就是特区嘛；中央没有钱，可以给些政策，你们自己去搞，杀出一条血路来。”

1992 年 1 月 18 日上午，邓小平的专列在武昌临时停车，湖北省和武汉市的领导同志前来迎接邓小平。小平同志对他们讲的第一句话就是：“以经济建设为中心，你们搞得怎么样啊？”小平话锋一转，说：“现在有一个问题，就是形式主义太多，电视打开尽是会议，会议多、文章长、讲话也太长，而且内容重复也多，新的语言不多。”他认为重要的话要讲，但要精简，形式主义也是官僚主义，要腾出时间来多办实事，多做实事，少说一点空话。说到这里，小平同志对着几位省领导嘱咐：“要把我的话转告中央，建议抓一下这个问题。”

在不到 30 分钟的讲话里，邓小平涉及的方面很多：“中国要警惕右，但主要是防止‘左’”；“建设速度能快就不要慢，低速度就等于停步，甚至等于后退”；“不坚持社会主义，不改革开放，不发展经济，不改善人民生活，只能是死路一条”；“现在要继续选人，选更年轻的同志帮助培养”……

29 分钟，邓小平几乎把南方谈话中所有的问题都点到了。

1992 年 1 月 20 日 9 时 25 分，在广东省、深圳市领导的陪同下，小平同志来到了深圳最高的国贸大厦。

1984 年小平同志来的时候，这座大厦正在兴建当中。53 层的大厦只用了 10 个月就建成了，三天建成一层楼，那是体现深圳速度的标志性建筑。进入国贸大厦，大厦员工们都挤在过道的两侧，“邓爷爷好！”的呼喊声和欢呼声响彻大厦的每个角落。

邓小平来到旋转餐厅，举目四望，浏览着深圳的全貌。

深圳市委书记李灏向小平同志汇报了本市经济发展状况。他说：“深圳的经济发展很快，人民生活水平不断提高。1984 年，全市月人均收入 600 元；截至 1991 年，人均收入增长到 2000 元……”

听到这个数字，小平同志很高兴，他说：“深圳的重要经验就是敢闯，没有一点‘闯’的精神，没有一点‘冒’的精神，就走不出一条新路，干不出一番新的事业。不冒点风险，办什么事情都有百分之百的把握，万无一失，谁敢说这样的话？”

在国贸大厦，小平同志边看边讲，声音时高时低，整整讲了 30 分钟。周围的同志都十分用心地听着，生怕漏掉一个字。脍炙人口的“发展才是硬道理”“坚持党的基本路线一百年不动摇”“两手抓，两手都要硬”以及三个“有利于”理论等，都是在这一年的这一天，从深圳的国贸大厦飞向全国的各个角落，飞向每一个中国人的心中。

邓小平喝了口水，继续说：“只有坚持这条路线，人民才会相信你、拥护你。谁要改变三中全会的路线、方针、政策，老百姓不答应，谁就会被打倒！”

1992 年小平同志视察南方，可以说是中国改革开放的重启，同党的十一届三中全会一样，是一次改变中国命运的历史性事件，是一次回暖人心的阳光之旅。

Lighting up the Way Forward

From January to February 1992, the 88-year-old Deng Xiaoping embarked on a southern tour with his family, the final large political act of his career. During the trip, he visited some of the Special Economic Zones that he had been instrumental in setting up in the early 1980s, and delivered a series of important remarks. “A planned economy is not equivalent to socialism, because there is planning under capitalism too; a market economy is not capitalism, because there are markets under socialism too.” “The crux of the matter is whether the road is capitalist or socialist. The chief criterion for making that judgement should be whether it promotes the growth of the productive forces in a socialist society, increases the overall strength of the socialist state and raises living standards.” “We should be bolder than before in conducting reform and opening-up to the outside and have the courage to experiment. We must not act like women with bound feet. Once we are sure that something should be done, we should dare to experiment and break a new path.” In what came to be known as the southern talks, Deng Xiaoping confirmed China’s commitment to reform and economic liberalization by summarizing the lessons and experience that the CPC had gained since the 3rd Plenary Session of the 11th Central Committee. The talks provided timely answers for many of the fundamental questions about China’s reform and opening-up, and freed people’s mind from old ideas by giving them new confidence. Emancipating people’s minds and seeking truth from facts, Deng Xiaoping’s southern talks revitalized China’s reform and opening-up and launched its socialist modernization into a new phase.

Deng Xiaoping had lighted up the way forward for China’s reform and opening-up at every critical juncture. The southern tour was his last significant contribution to China’s development, as well as his enduring legacy as the “Architect of Modern China”.

As I followed Deng Xiaoping on his tour, one message had been repeated in each of the places he visited, “It was my idea to set up the Special Economic Zones, and it was approved by the Central Committee. Whether it succeeds or not, I have to see for myself.”

As early as April 1979, during the Central Work Conference, Deng Xiaoping had told Xi

Zhongxun and Yang Shangkun, who were then Guangdong's top officials, about his plan to establish the SEZs. Deng said, "It's a good idea to call it the 'special zone'; after all, the Shaan-Gan-Ning Border Region used to be a special zone! If the central government cannot help with money, at least it can help with policy; then you can go figure it out on your own, you can blaze your own trail."

Deng Xiaoping's train pulled into Wuchang station for a stopover on the morning of January 18, 1992, where he met with the top officials from Hubei and Wuhan. The first thing Deng said was, "How are you doing in terms of economic development, the center of everything else?" Then he switched the subject to the problem of formalism, "Every time you turn on the TV, you see a meeting being held. We hold way too many meetings, and our articles and speeches are too long and too redundant, in both content and language." As far as Deng Xiaoping was concerned, some important words have to be repeated, but in a concise way, as he said, "Formalism is a kind of bureaucratism. We should spend more time on practical matters. That means saying less and doing more." Deng also asked the local officials to pass on his word to the central government, so that something could be done about this problem.

In a speech that lasted less than half an hour, Deng Xiaoping touched upon almost all the important points he wanted to make. "China should maintain vigilance against the Right but primarily against the 'Left'." "Where local conditions permit, development should proceed as fast as possible", because "slow growth equals stagnation and even retrogression." "If we did not adhere to socialism, implement the policies of reform and opening-up to the outside world, develop the economy and raise living standards, we would find ourselves in a blind alley." "More young people should be promoted to positions of leadership."...

The 29-minute speech almost covered all the important topics of Deng Xiaoping's southern talks.

At 9:25 on January 20, 1992, Deng Xiaoping arrived at the Guomao Building, the tallest skyscraper in Shenzhen at the time.

The building was still under construction when Deng Xiaoping visited Shenzhen in 1984. The 53-floor office tower only took 10 months to build, which earned the city's rapid development the nickname "Shenzhen speed". Large crowds had lined up on both sides of the corridor, and excited shouts and cheers of "Hello, Grandpa Deng" greeted Deng Xiaoping as he entered the building.

During the tour, Deng Xiaoping came to the revolving restaurant, where he had a bird's-eye view of Shenzhen's cityscape.

Li Hao, then secretary of the CPC Shenzhen Municipal Committee, reported to Deng Xiaoping about the city's economic development. "Shenzhen's economy is developing rapidly and people's living standards are rising. The city's monthly per capita income was 600 yuan in

1984, while that number has increased to 2,000 yuan by 1991."

Upon learning this good news, Deng Xiaoping was truly happy, as he said, "That is the important lesson to be learned from Shenzhen. If we don't have such pioneering spirit, if we're too afraid to take risks, if we have no energy and drive, we cannot break a new path, or accomplish anything new. Who dares to say that he is 100% guaranteed to succeed and that he is taking no risks?"

During his tour of the Guomao Building, Deng Xiaoping talked a lot while he walked around. For a whole half hour, everyone present paid close attention to everything Deng had to say. "Development is of overriding importance." "We should adhere to the basic line for a hundred years, with no vacillation." "China must grab with both hands, grasping firmly with both." All these famous sayings, including the three criteria for judging whether the road is capitalist or socialist, would soon be heard and heeded by every Chinese.

After taking a sip of water, Deng Xiaoping continued, "We must adhere to the basic line. That is the only way to win the trust and support of the people. Anyone who attempted to change the line, principles and policies adopted since the 3rd Plenary Session of the 11th Central Committee would not be countenanced by the people; he would be toppled!"

Deng Xiaoping's 1992 southern tour had revitalized China's reform and opening-up, won over people's support and confidence, and changed the course of Chinese history forever. Its historic significance is arguably only rivaled by the 3rd Plenary Session of the 11th Central Committee of the CPC.

邓小平巨幅彩色画像

在深圳的闹市区，深南大道与红岭路交汇的西北侧，赫然矗立着一幅高 10 米、长 30 米的邓小平视察深圳的巨幅画像。身着中山装的邓小平面带微笑，目光坚定地凝视前方。在画面的左上方，就是小平同志视察深圳时讲的那句著名的“坚持党的基本路线一百年不动摇”14 个大字。

这幅画像是根据 1984 年小平同志视察深圳时我拍的一幅肖像照临摹绘制的。那是我们终生不能忘怀的老人家第一次南方视察的火红年代。

历史给了深圳一次这样特别的机会，让来来往往的人们能够瞻仰改革开放总设计师的伟人风采，体会他高瞻远瞩的战略思想。这幅巨幅画像自 1992 年 9 月落成后，受到深圳人民的格外关爱，这是小平同志推动改革开放的形象见证，也是深圳历史上辉煌的地标性建筑，吸引着来自四面八方的中外游客。

Deng Xiaoping's Portrait in Shenzhen

The iconic 10-meter-tall, 30-meter-wide portrait of Deng Xiaoping stands in a square at the northwest side of the intersection of Shennan Boulevard and Hongling Road in the downtown area of Shenzhen. The image shows Deng Xiaoping, dressed in a Mao suit, smiling and firmly looking ahead. Deng Xiaoping's famous quotation during his tour of Shenzhen is inscribed in the upper-left corner of the portrait, "We should adhere to the basic line for a hundred years, with no vacillation."

The portrait was copied and created from a photo I took of Deng Xiaoping during his visit to Shenzhen in 1984. It had captured the historic significance of Deng's first southern tour that none of us would ever forget.

The portrait stands as a historical testament to Deng Xiaoping's contribution as the chief architect of China's reform and opening-up. It is a symbol for his wisdom, vision and leadership in building socialism with Chinese characteristics. Since its completion in September 1992, it has provided a unique opportunity for people from all around the world to appreciate the historical connection between Deng Xiaoping and Shenzhen.

坚持党的基本路线
一百年不动摇
SANTANA LX

叶剑英元帅（右一）与习仲勋（中）、杨尚昆（左一）亲切握手。

Marshal Ye Jianying (first from right) shaking hands with Xi Zhongxun (center) and Yang Shangkun (first from left).

两位书记迎接叶帅

1979 年 2 月，时任全国人大常务委员会委员长的叶剑英元帅回到故乡广州休假。广东省委第一书记习仲勋、第二书记杨尚昆到白云机场迎接叶帅。老战友相聚，非常开心，叶帅同时拉着习仲勋、杨尚昆的手，高兴地说：“广东的改革开放，就要看你们的哟！”

十一届三中全会以后，中央把改革开放的突破口选在广东。在确定领导人时，叶剑英元帅力荐习仲勋、杨尚昆，他说：“派出他们这两位资格老、吨位重、曾担任过中央重要职务的干部到广东，就是因为广东问题复杂，他们两个可以压得住阵。”

习仲勋、杨尚昆在看望叶帅时，把广东准备先走一步，建立一些经济开发区，希望中央能给一些政策的想法向叶帅报告了，叶剑英非常赞同，鼓励他们说：“你们马上去北京，当面向小平同志汇报，争取早些得到中央的支持。”1979 年 4 月，参加中央工作会议的习仲勋当面向邓小平、叶剑英汇报了广东的工作思路，邓小平说：“还是叫特区好，陕甘宁就是特区嘛！”为了让经济特区各项政策有法可依，1980 年春，叶剑英要求习仲勋、杨尚昆尽快拟出经济特区条例，呈报国务院和全国人大常委会。1980 年 8 月，全国人大常委会批准了《广东省经济特区条例》。

Two Party Secretaries Shaking Hands with Marshal Ye Jianying

In February 1979, Marshal Ye Jianying, then Chairman of the Standing Committee of the National People's Congress, returned to his hometown of Guangzhou for vacation. Xi Zhongxun, then First Secretary of the CPC Guangdong Provincial Committee, and Yang Shangkun, then Second Secretary of the CPC Guangdong Provincial Committee, went to the Baiyun International Airport to welcome Marshal Ye. Having been good friends and old comrades during the revolution, the three of them were happy to meet again. Feeling truly excited, Marshal Ye took the hands of both Xi Zhongxun and Yang Shangkun and told them, "The reform and opening-up in Guangdong now depend on you guys!"

After the 3rd Plenary Session of the 11th Central Committee, the central government decided to choose Guangdong as the starting point of the country's reform and opening-up. During high-level deliberations over the choice of leaders for Guangdong, Marshal Ye strongly recommended Xi Zhongxun and Yang Shangkun, because he believed that "Both of them have held top positions in the central government, and they also have the prestige and qualifications to govern Guangdong, especially in light of the complicated situation there."

When Xi Zhongxun and Yang Shangkun visited Marshal Ye, they shared with him their idea to set up a few economic development zones in Guangdong first, and their wish for the central government to provide them with policy incentives. Ye Jianying highly approved of their proposal, and encouraged them to go to Beijing immediately, and "report this to Comrade Xiaoping in person and try to get the support from the central government as early as possible." While he was attending the Central Work Conference held in April 1979, Xi Zhongxun reported to Deng Xiaoping and Ye Jianying in person about his plan for promoting economic development in Guangdong. Deng responded by saying, "It's a good idea to call it the 'special zone'; after all, the Shaan-Gan-Ning Border Region used to be a special zone!" To establish the legal basis for setting up and regulating the Special Economic Zones, Ye Jianying told Xi Zhongxun and Yang Shangkun to draft regulations on this matter, and then submit them to the State Council and the Standing Committee of the National People's Congress for approval. As a result, the Regulations on Special Economic Zones in Guangdong Province was approved by the Standing Committee of the NPC in August 1980.

杨尚昆（左）、任仲夷（右）和广东省委领导去机场迎接自北京归来的习仲勋（中）。

Yang Shangkun (left), Ren Zhongyi (right) and leaders of the CPC Guangdong Provincial Committee welcomed Xi Zhongxun (center), who had just flown back from Beijing.

改革开放的接力棒

1980 年 11 月，习仲勋、杨尚昆相继从广东调回中央工作，任仲夷从辽宁省委书记任上接棒成为广东省委第一书记。习仲勋、杨尚昆离任前请示中央，再给广东一些更为宽松的政策。9 月 28 日，中央专门下发会议纪要，清楚写明："中央授权给广东省，对中央各部门的指令和要求采取灵活办法。适合的就执行，不适合的可以不执行或变通办理。"这个纪要的核心内容，是小平同志拍板决定的。

任仲夷赴任后，团结和带领广东省委班子，率领全省广大干部群众，在中央改革开放的总方针和经济发展的总体规划下，大胆探索，积极实践，把党的方针政策与广东的实际情况结合起来，创造性地贯彻执行，克服了重重困难，经受了严峻考验，为探索广东的改革开放和在全国先行一步做出了重大贡献。

习仲勋从广东离任前夕，受中央之命，于 1980 年 10 月率省长代表团出国访问。访问结束回京报告完毕，又乘飞机回到广东。

The Torch Relay of the Reform and Opening-up in Guangdong

In November 1980, Xi Zhongxun and Yang Shangkun returned from Guangdong to Beijing to work for the central government, while Ren Zhongyi took over as the First Secretary of the CPC Guangdong Provincial Committee. Before their departure, Xi Zhongxun and Yang Shangkun asked the central government to give Guangdong more policy leeway. On September 28, the central government issued minutes of a meeting which clearly stated that, "The central government authorizes Guangdong Province to adopt a flexible approach in fulfilling the instructions and requirements of the central ministries and departments. Guangdong is allowed a high degree of freedom in deciding the extent to which it shall follow the orders from the central government." Actually, it was Deng Xiaoping who authorized the core content of the minutes.

The change of leadership did not slow Guangdong from further development and achieving new accomplishments. As the successor of Xi Zhongxun and Yang Shangkun, Ren Zhongyi had led the cadres and masses of Guangdong to overcome challenges and obstacles, and made great contributions to the success of Guangdong as the exemplary of China's reform and opening-up.

In October 1980, on the eve of his departure from Guangdong, Xi Zhongxun was appointed by the central government to lead a delegation of provincial governors on a visit abroad. After finishing the trip and returning to Beijing for a briefing, he flew back to Guangdong.

邓小平（左一）与杨尚昆（左二）、王震（左三）在专列上。

Deng Xiaoping (first from left) with Yang Shangkun (second from left) and Wang Zhen (third from left) on a train.

邓小平与王震、杨尚昆在专列上

1984 年，中国的改革开放已经进行到第七个年头。广东的那几个经济特区搞得到底怎么样？邓小平同志决定亲自到实地看一看。

1 月 22 日，小平同志坐上南下的火车，前往深圳、珠海、厦门等经济特区实地考察。陪同小平同志视察的，有时任国务院副总理王震同志、中央军委副主席杨尚昆同志。王震、杨尚昆与小平同志有着半个多世纪的战斗友谊，他们都是共和国历史上叱咤风云的人物。十一届三中全会刚闭幕，中央就把杨尚昆派到广东，与习仲勋同志共同实践改革开放的战略目标。为了建设几个经济特区，习仲勋、杨尚昆两位老革命家倾注了大量心血。在专列的餐厅里，小平同志对杨尚昆说："到了你的老根据地了，不要叫我们迷路哟。"杨尚昆笑了笑说："特区一直在你心里嘛，不会迷路的。"

Deng Xiaoping Having a Conversation with Wang Zhen and Yang Shangkun on the Train

China's reform and opening-up was already in its seventh year in 1984. In order to check on the actual development of the Special Economic Zones in Guangdong, Deng Xiaoping embarked on his first southern tour.

On January 22, Deng Xiaoping boarded a southbound train and began his trip to Shenzhen, Zhuhai, Xiamen and other Special Economic Zones. Wang Zhen, then Vice Premier of the State Council, and Yang Shangkun, then Vice Chairman of the Central Military Commission, accompanied Deng on this trip. The friendship of the three leaders can be traced back to more than fifty years ago, as they had worked and fought together during the Chinese revolution. Immediately following the 3rd Plenary Session of the 11th Central Committee, Yang Shangkun was appointed by the central government to go to Guangdong and work with Xi Zhongxun to put Deng's ideas of reform and opening-up into practice. Both Xi Zhongxun and Yang Shangkun had committed themselves to the establishment of the Special Economic Zones in Guangdong. In the dining car, Deng Xiaoping jokingly said to Yang Shangkun, "Guangdong is your home base, I hope we won't get lost there." Yang Shangkun smiled and said, "You won't get lost at all, because the Special Economic Zones are always on your mind."

第一次视察深圳

1984 年，我国的改革开放遇到了一些困难和问题，特别是围绕特区经济建设碰到的一些问题出现了一些议论，并有越来越严重的趋势。在这个重要关头，改革开放的总设计师邓小平开始了去南方视察之旅，对南方的几个经济特区进行实地考察。

1 月 24 日中午，小平同志乘坐专列抵达深圳。小平同志身穿灰色中山装，脚穿黑色皮鞋，红光满面，步履稳健地走下火车，同迎候在车站月台上的深圳市领导人一一握手。

市委书记梁湘按捺不住内心的喜悦，在车站月台上就向小平同志汇报，他说办特区这几年来工农业产值、财政收入增长幅度很大、速度很快，特别是工业产值，1982 年达到 3.6 亿元，1983 年跃上 7.2 亿元。这时小平插话说："那就是一年翻了一番了？"梁湘回答道："是翻了一番，比建特区前的 1978 年增长了 10 倍多！"邓小平满意地点了点头。

Deng Xiaoping's First Inspection Tour of Shenzhen

In 1984, China's reform and opening-up had encountered many challenges and problems, especially as the controversy over the nature of the Special Economic Zones began to grow more serious. It was at this critical juncture that Deng Xiaoping embarked on a southern tour as the chief architect of China's reform program, so he could check for himself how the Special Economic Zones were doing.

At noon on January 24, Deng Xiaoping arrived at the Shenzhen Railway Station. Dressed in a gray Mao suit and black leather shoes, he looked full of energy. After he got off the train, he was immediately greeted by the leaders of the Shenzhen government.

Liang Xiang, then secretary of the CPC Shenzhen Municipal Committee, could not wait to share with Deng Xiaoping the achievements of Shenzhen's development. Liang told Deng that Shenzhen's industrial and agricultural output value and fiscal revenues had increased rapidly in the past few years. In particular, the city's industrial output value had reached 360 million yuan in 1982 and then jumped to 720 million yuan in 1983. "So, the number has doubled in just over a year?" Deng Xiaoping asked. "Not just doubled, it has actually been a ten-fold increase since 1978, before the establishment of the SEZ." Liang Xiang replied. Upon hearing this, Deng Xiaoping nodded with great satisfaction.

梁湘（左）在车站迎候邓小平。

Liang Xiang (left) greeting Deng Xiaoping at the Shenzhen Railway Station.

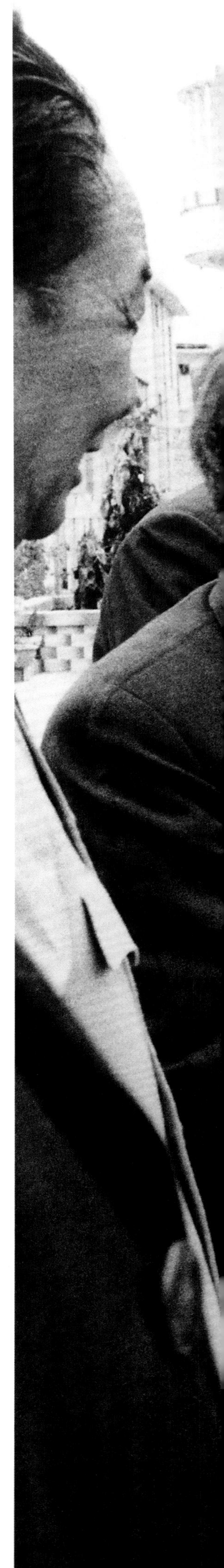

1984 年 1 月 25 日，邓小平视察广东省首个“万元户村”。

On January 25, 1984, Deng Xiaoping inspected the first “wanyuanhu” village in Guangdong.

到访“万元户村”

1984 年 1 月 25 日 10 时 30 分，刚从中航技术进出口公司视察完毕的邓小平，又踏进了渔村。陪同小平视察的深圳市委书记梁湘汇报说，这个村与香港仅一河之隔，是名副其实的改革开放前沿阵地。全村渔民在改革开放政策引领下，奋发图强，通过几年的拼搏，全村的面貌发生了重大改变，1981 年全村家家都成了“万元户”，是全省首个“万元户村”。“万元户”在当时是富裕户的代名词，成为全国经济发展的排头兵，“万元户村”更是改革开放催生的新生事物。

渔民新村党支部书记吴柏森在村口迎候邓小平，邓小平高兴地和他握手。吴柏森走在前边引路，兴奋而又自豪地介绍自改革开放短短几年来，乡村建设发展和老百姓生活发生的变化。首先映入小平同志眼帘的，是平坦、宽阔、整洁的街道，还有街道两旁一排排、一幢幢两层高的小别墅。“邓伯伯，到我家坐坐吧。”吴柏森热情地邀请邓小平，小平同志欣然应允。

这是一幢面积 180 多平方米的别墅式小楼，有六室两厅，屋顶装着吊扇，地面全用防滑地板瓷铺就。客厅的墙壁上悬挂着风景壁画，沙发、彩电、音响等时髦用品应有尽有；厨房干净整洁，电冰箱、电子煤气炉、不锈钢炊具一应俱全；吴柏森还领着小平同志参观了娱乐室、健身室，在健身室的乒乓球桌上，小平拿起一只球拍掂了掂，微微一笑。所有房间都转了一遍，小平同志看得非常高兴，他问吴柏森：“每个家庭都有这些吗？”“都有了，都有了。我们穷苦了多少年的渔民，做梦也没有想到能过上今天这样的好日子！感谢邓伯伯为我们制定了这么好的政策。”小平同志摆了摆手，认真地说：“要感谢党中央！”

小平同志问吴柏森，全村人平均月收入有多少，吴柏森告诉他，全村人均月收入 430 多元。这时小平的三女儿邓榕贴着他的耳朵，小声地说：“比您的工资还高呢！”小平呵呵一笑，高兴地重复道：“比我的工资还高呢！全国要都像这样还得 100 年。”

小平同志问老百姓还有什么要求，吴柏森说：“外界有人说我们这里是搞资本主义，大家担心以后政策再变回去。”小平听罢哈哈大笑，郑重地对吴柏森说：“能让老百姓共同富裕的政策凭啥子要变？如果说要变，只能是越变越好嘛！”小平的话音刚落，立即响起一阵热烈的掌声。

Visiting the Village of "Wanyuanhu"

Deng Xiaoping had a tight schedule during his Shenzhen tour. On January 25, he first paid a visit to the China National Aero-Technology Import & Export Corporation, and then arrived at a fishing village. He was told by Liang Xiang, secretary of the CPC Shenzhen Municipal Committee, that this village was literally at the frontline of the reform and opening-up, as it was just a river away from Hong Kong. Encouraged by the reform policies, the village's fishermen had strived to change their own lives for the better. Thanks to their hard work over the last few years, every family in the village had become "wanyuanhu" by 1981 ("wanyuanhu" in Chinese means a household with an annual income of over 10,000 yuan), and the village itself had become the first "wanyuanhu" village in Guangdong. At that time, "wanyuanhu" was synonymous with wealth and economic development, and the birth of "wanyuanhu" villages like this one was testimony to the success of the reform and opening-up policy.

At the entrance of the Fishermen's New Village, Deng Xiaoping was greeted by Wu Baisen, secretary of the village's CPC Branch Committee and Deng's tour guide for the day. During the village tour, Wu Baisen proudly shared with Deng Xiaoping the great changes that had happened to the village and its people in just a few years since the reform and opening-up. Along the way, Deng Xiaoping saw wide and clean streets, and rows of two-story villas on both sides. Wu Baisen warmly invited Deng Xiaoping to visit his house, and Deng readily agreed.

Wu Baisen's house was a villa-style building of more than 180 square meters. With six rooms and two halls, it was nicely decorated and fully furnished with all the modern home appliances. It even got an entertainment room as well as a fitness room with its own table tennis table. Deng Xiaoping took great interest in this beautiful house and went into all the rooms. After finishing his tour with excitement, Deng asked Wu, "Does every family in the village have what you have?" "Of course, every family is the same! We used to be really impoverished fishermen, and we never dreamed that we could one day live such a good life! It is all because of you, Uncle Deng, who came through with such good policy for us!" Waving his hand as if to disagree, Deng Xiaoping replied, "You should be grateful to the CPC Central Committee, not me!"

Deng Xiaoping then asked Wu Baisen about the average monthly income of the villagers, and was told that the average villager now made more than 430 yuan every month. Deng Rong, Deng's third daughter, whispered to her father, "It's even higher than your salary!" Laughing happily, Deng Xiaoping repeated his daughter's words, "It's even higher than my salary! It will probably take another 100 years before the whole country becomes like this."

When asked by Deng Xiaoping if they had any other concerns, Wu Baisen replied, "There are people out there who call our village taking the capitalist road, so we worry that there might be a reversal in future policy." Laughing out loud, Deng Xiaoping made a promise to Wu Baisen, "Why should we change the policy that will make everyone rich? If there's going to be changes, it will only be changes for the better!" Deng Xiaoping's words was received with a big round of applause.

渔村村委会

从村党支部书记吴柏森家出来，在市、镇、村领导干部的陪同下，小平同志来到渔民新村村委会视察。

村委会建得不错。院子四周装了许多健身器材，办公室、会议室、活动室、文化室、荣誉室宽敞明亮，荣誉室的墙壁上还挂了许多锦旗、奖牌和奖状。在村委会院内看了一圈，小平同志对干部们说：“这里的物质文明先进，精神文明也很好嘛！”

At the CPC Village Committee

After finishing the tour of Wu Baisen's house, the next stop was the village's party committee.

The office of the village's party committee was well built, with various rooms for business and pleasure as well as many fitness equipment. There was one special room that was decorated with banners, medals and awards. After finishing the tour, Deng Xiaoping praised the village cadres, "You have done a good job advancing the material standards as well as the cultural and ethical standards here!"

喜看“深圳速度”

蛇口，是建设深圳经济特区的出发地。1979 年，交通部驻香港招商局的袁庚回到蛇口组建工业区，经过几年奋斗，把一片渺无人烟的荒滩建成中国第一个外向型经济开发区。

1984 年 1 月 26 日，邓小平来到了蛇口工业区。在深圳市委书记梁湘等人的陪同下，小平同志登上了刚建成的 20 层国际商业大厦的楼顶，眺望这里的建设场景。远处，60 多幢 18 层以上的高楼平地而起，有的已经竣工，有的正在建设中。正在施工中的世贸大楼，三天就能盖一层，创造了令人瞩目的“深圳速度”。小平同志沿着楼顶边沿四下眺望，无限欣喜，他边走边说：“我都看见了，都看清楚了。”

Impressed by the Shenzhen Speed

Starting from a geographically limited area, Shekou later became the template for Deng Xiaoping's subsequent policy to establish China's Special Economic Zones. With the support from China's Ministry of Transport, Yuan Geng prepared a pilot project for Shekou in the form of an industrial zone, and managed to transform it into China's very first export-oriented economic development zone.

Deng Xiaoping paid a visit to the Shekou Industrial Zone on January 26, 1984. He climbed to the roof of the newly completed 20-story International Commerce Building, and took a bird's-eye view of the construction work around the building. Here and there, high-rise buildings sprung up one after another. As skyscrapers like the International Trade Tower were being built at the speed of one floor in three days, Deng Xiaoping witnessed the famous "Shenzhen Speed" in person, and endorsed it as a development model. Looking down from the top of the building, Deng Xiaoping was filled with joy, "I've seen it all, I've seen everything clearly."

梁湘（右三）、梁灵光（左一）陪同邓小平登上国际商业大厦楼顶。

Liang Xiang (third from right) and Liang Lingguang (first from left) accompanying Deng Xiaoping to the roof of the International Commerce Building.

邓小平听取袁庚的汇报。（前排自左至右：杨尚昆、邓小平、袁庚、王震）

Deng Xiaoping listening to Yuan Geng's report. (front row, from left to right: Yang Shangkun, Deng Xiaoping, Yuan Geng, Wang Zhen)

在蛇口工业区听取袁庚汇报

在深圳蛇口港的路旁绿地上，矗立着一块醒目的棕红色标语牌，上面写有 12 个金色大字："时间就是金钱，效率就是生命。"这条传遍全国的标语，出自蛇口工业区管委会主任袁庚之口。

1984 年 1 月 26 日，邓小平来到深圳蛇口工业区视察，恰遇袁庚负责接待。老人家早先就从李先念、谷牧等中央领导同志嘴里听到过他的名字。小平同志一行饶有兴致地听取了工业区发展的曲折经历，以及短短几年取得的重大成果。简单介绍完毕，袁庚就带着小平等领导同志登上微波通讯站的两层小楼。站在楼顶，远眺蛇口已经建立起来的合资工厂和直岸式码头，远处那块标语牌也赫然映入小平的眼帘。小平指着标语牌，问道："那是你的专利喽？""算是吧。我们当初提出这句口号时，有许多人反对，说这是资本主义的口号，竖起的标语牌几次被人拆下。我们始终坚信，我们讲的是实话，这是改革开放的口号。"小平听了点了点头，说："对头。"得到小平同志的首肯，袁庚又继续汇报了从打破大锅饭到招商引资、从住房商品化再到全国人才招聘等情况，从 1979 年到 1984 年 5 年多时间里，蛇口创造了 24 项全国第一。

袁庚又指着眼前这座两层高的小洋楼，告诉小平："这是蛇口刚建立不久的微波通讯站，里边的设备全是从国外进口的。微波通讯系统的建立，解决了蛇口的通讯问题，搭起了沟通境外的桥梁。"小平看得十分认真，听得特别入神。

袁庚颇有感触地对小平说："蛇口工业区的机遇来之不易，如果慢慢腾腾地搞，啥也做不成。我们虽然取得了一些成绩，但到现在还有人骂我们是'资本主义的冒险家'。"小平同志听罢微微一笑，说："没有点儿冒险精神啥子事情也做不成，你们是改革开放的冒险家！"说这句话的时候，小平的声音很大。

Receiving a Briefing from Yuan Geng at the Shekou Industrial Zone

Yuan Geng, a pioneer of unprecedented reform policies during the 1980s, coined the widely-known slogan"time is gold and efficiency is life" in 1981. It was endorsed by Deng Xiaoping during his visit to Shenzhen in January 1984. As a motto of China's reform era, the slogan has been inscribed on a giant billboard in Shekou.

On January 26, 1984, Deng Xiaoping inspected the Shekou Industrial Zone, where he was received by Yuan Geng. Deng had heard of Yuan's story for a while from CPC leaders such as Li Xiannian and Gu Mu. Deng Xiaoping listened with great interest to Yuan Geng's introduction to the development and achievements of the industrial zone over the last few years. After the introduction, Yuan Geng led Deng Xiaoping and other leaders up to the top roof of a microwave tower, where the joint venture factories and container terminals that Shekou was famous for could be seen from afar. The billboard with the inscription of Yuan Geng's famous slogan caught Deng Xiaoping's attention. "I assume that was your invention?" Deng Xiaoping asked Yuan Geng. "Well, sort of. When we first put forward this slogan, there was a lot of opposition, some even calling it a capitalist slogan. Even the placard had to be taken off several times. However, we always have faith in what we stand for, we believe it is the slogan of the reform and opening-up." "You're absolutely right." Deng Xiaoping nodded with approval. With Deng Xiaoping's support and encouragement, Yuan Geng went on to share the policies that he had pioneered in Shekou, such as merit-based recruitment, promotion and pay, open access to housing, and attracting foreign direct investors. Deng Xiaoping was truly impressed when he learned that Shekou had broken twenty-four national records from 1979 to 1984.

Pointing to the two-story building in front, Yuan Geng told Deng Xiaoping, "This is our newly-built microwave communications tower, and all the equipment inside are imported from abroad. The establishment of this microwave system has solved the communication problems for Shekou, and now we have a bridge of contacts with the outside world." Deng Xiaoping paid great attention to everything Yuan Geng had said.

During the tour, Yuan Geng got a bit emotional when he expressed his concerns to Deng Xiaoping, "The development opportunity of the Shekou Industrial Zone did not come by easily. In fact, we would've achieved nothing if we had taken things slowly. Despite our accomplishments, however, some people still denounce us as 'capitalist adventurers' even today." Deng Xiaoping replied with a smile, "Nothing can be achieved without a bit of adventurous spirit. I would call you the adventurers of reform and opening-up!" As a matter of fact, Deng raised his voice quite a bit when he made this comment.

告别蛇口工业区

作为改革开放初期就开发建设起来，而后成为国家级开放口岸的蛇口工业区，深深吸引了邓小平、王震、杨尚昆三位老革命家。他们共同赞扬开发区领导人袁庚所提出的"时间就是金钱，效率就是生命"的改革开放口号。

1984 年 1 月 26 日，小平同志结束了对深圳的视察，准备从蛇口出发去往珠海经济特区继续考察。深圳市委和蛇口工业区的领导在蛇口军港码头为邓小平等中央领导送行。

Bidding Farewell to the Shekou Industrial Zone

The success of the Shekou Industrial Zone at the beginning of China's reform era had deeply impressed Deng Xiaoping, Wang Zhen and Yang Shangkun, three seasoned revolutionaries. They had unanimously endorsed the reform slogan of "time is gold and efficiency is life" proposed by Yuan Geng, known as "Father of Shekou".

On January 26, 1984, after finishing his inspection of Shenzhen, Deng Xiaoping was ready to leave Shekou for the Zhuhai Special Economic Zone to continue his tour. The leaders of the Shenzhen Municipal Committee and the Shekou Industrial Zone bid their farewell to Deng Xiaoping and other leaders of the central government at the Shekou Military Port.

1984年1月26日，邓小平、王震（二排右三）、杨尚昆（二排左三）在深圳蛇口和海军某部官兵合影。

Deng Xiaoping, Wang Zhen (second row, third from right) and Yang Shangkun (second row, third from left) taking a photo with officers and soldiers of the Chinese navy in Shekou, Shenzhen on January 26, 1984.

乘军舰去珠海

1984年1月26日14时45分，小平同志结束了对深圳的视察，从蛇口军港乘坐边防军679号舰和674号舰，前往珠海视察。深圳市委书记梁湘在军港为小平同志送行，广东省省长梁灵光和其他一些领导同志来到军港码头陪同小平同志去珠海。

军舰上，全体海军官兵整齐列队，迎接共和国军队的最高统帅。

Going to Zhuhai on a Warship

After ending his inspection tour of Shenzhen on January 26, 1984, Deng Xiaoping boarded a guard ship from the Shekou military port, and headed for Zhuhai to continue his tour. Liang Xiang, then secretary of the CPC Shenzhen Municipal Committee, saw Deng Xiaoping off at the port, while Liang Lingguang, then Governor of Guangdong, and some other top officials joined Deng's tour and went to Zhuhai with him.

On board the warship, the naval officers lined up to greet Deng Xiaoping, the commander-in-chief of the People's Republic of China.

梁灵光（左三）陪同邓小平去珠海。（左二为柯平，左四为梁广大）
Liang Lingguang (third from left) accompanying Deng Xiaoping during his trip to Zhuhai. (second from left, Ke Ping; fourth from left, Liang Guangda)

吴健民（右二）、梁广大（右一）迎候邓小平。

Wu Jianmin (second from right) and Liang Guangda (first from right) greeting Deng Xiaoping.

珠海市委领导迎接邓小平

1984 年 1 月 29 日，小平同志从中山乘车来到珠海视察，市委书记吴健民、代市长梁广大早就在市政府大门口迎候小平同志。吴健民书记说：“珠海人民热烈欢迎您！”梁广大代市长说：“珠海人民盼您盼了五年了！”

1984 年 1 月 29 日，邓小平、王震（右二）、杨尚昆（右三）和珠海市的领导同志在珠海狮山电子厂视察。

On January 29, 1984, Deng Xiaoping, Wang Zhen (second from right), Yang Shangkun (third from right) and the top officials of Zhuhai inspected the Shishan Electronics Factory.

Greeted by the Leaders of the CPC Zhuhai Municipal Committee

On January 29, 1984, Deng Xiaoping left Zhongshan for Zhuhai, his next destination. He was warmly greeted by Wu Jianmin, then secretary of the CPC Zhuhai Municipal Committee, and Liang Guangda, then acting mayor of Zhuhai, at the gate of the municipal government. Wu Jianmin said to Deng Xiaoping, "The people of Zhuhai warmly welcome you!" Liang Guangda added, "The people of Zhuhai have been looking forward to your visit for five years!"

参观生产录音机的工厂

录音机，是 20 世纪 80 年代的年轻人梦寐以求的时髦物件。当年的中国内地，文娱生活相当匮乏，改革开放后，看到港澳青年提着单卡录音机，边走边听流行歌曲，内地青年羡慕极了。

买一台吗？没钱。即使攒够了钱，商场里也没货。

内地第一家生产录音机的工厂在珠海应运而生。巨大的市场需求，给经营者带来丰厚的利润，也给工厂带来辉煌的前景。

1984 年 1 月，小平同志在珠海市委书记吴健民等同志的陪同下视察了这家工厂。技术人员向他详细介绍了产品性能，管理人员向他汇报了产品的经销情况，小平同志听得十分仔细，不时地向技术人员、管理人员询问原料来源、技术来源、工人的工资福利待遇等细节问题，表现出对新兴的民营企业的特别的关心。

Visiting a Tape Recorder Factory

Every young man in the chinese mainland in the 1980s would dream for a tape recorder, which was a symbol of fashion at the time. After years of isolation, the chinese mainland had been deprived of almost all forms of entertainment. With the reform and opening-up, young people from the Chinese mainland desired to enjoy the same lifestyle as their counterparts from Hong Kong and Macau, who were often seen carrying a portable tape recorder and listening to pop music.

Even if you had saved enough money and tried to buy a tape recorder for yourself, it was impossible because the department stores were always out of stock.

The chinese mainland first tape recorder factory was soon born in Zhuhai to meet the enormous market demand. It became an immediate success, growing rapidly and generating huge profits for its owners.

Deng Xiaoping visited this factory in January 1984, accompanied by Wu Jianmin, secretary of the CPC Zhuhai Municipal Committee, and other local cadres. He listened carefully to detailed reports about the function and marketing of the product, while making inquiries regarding its source of raw materials and technology as well as the workers' salaries and benefits. Everyone could see that Deng had a special concern for China's emerging private enterprises.

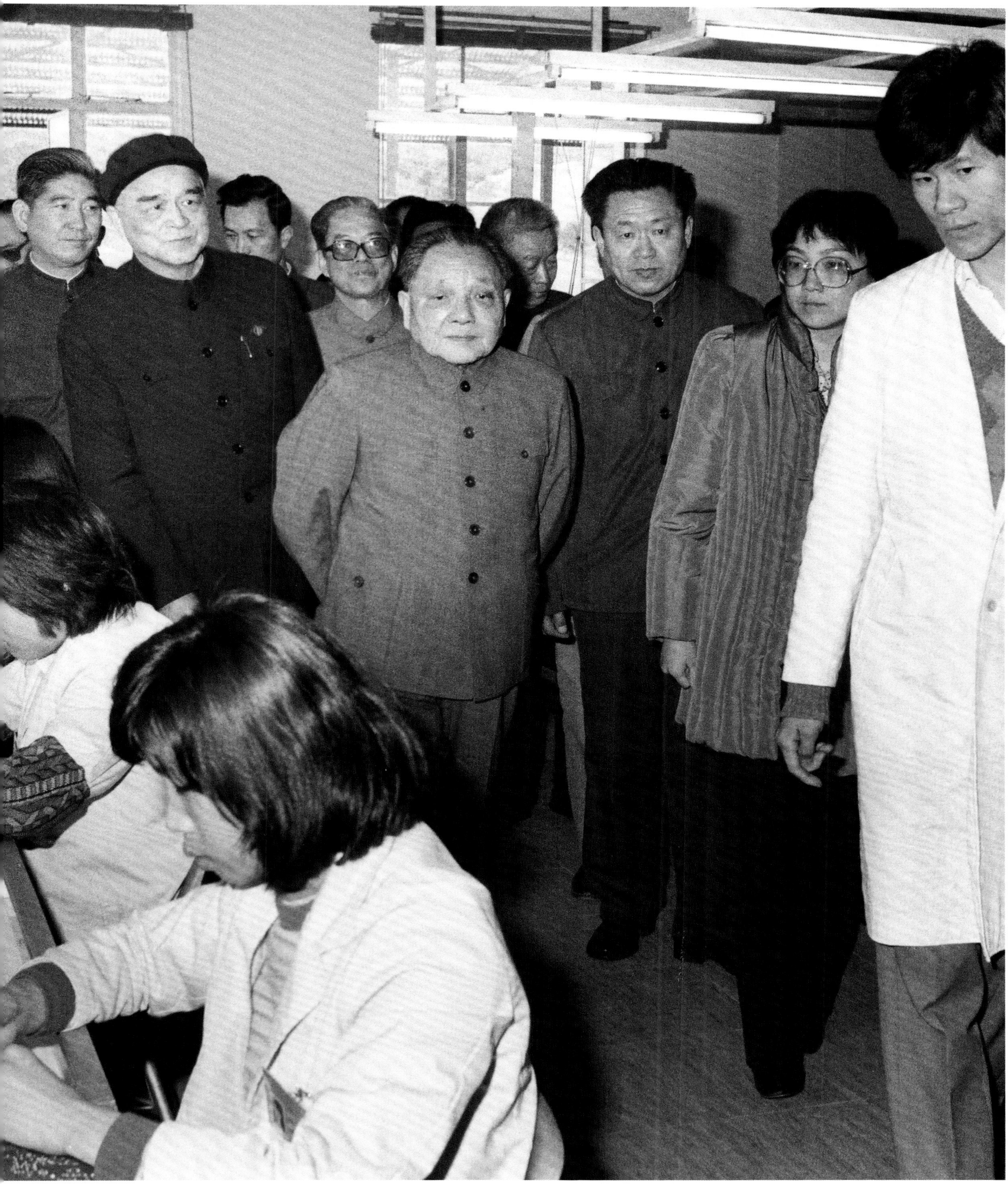

与霍英东、马万祺亲切交谈

1984 年 1 月，小平同志视察中山，恰逢霍英东捐资兴建的中山温泉宾馆开业。28 日晚，小平同志在宾馆同专程赶来与他见面的霍英东（中国香港）、马万祺（中国澳门）以及澳门南光公司的代表等亲切会面。小平同志信心满满地说：“办特区是我倡议的，中央批准的，中山的发展势头很好，路子走对了。”霍英东高兴地称赞道：“这政策是对头的。”邓小平又同他们谈起了改革开放，谈起了即将回归的香港和澳门，期望他们抓住机遇，继续配合中央政府，坚持改革开放，为香港、澳门的回归做贡献。

A Friendly Conversation with Fok Ying Tung and Ma Man-kei

During Deng Xiaoping's inspection tour of Zhongshan in January 1984, he learned about the opening of the Zhongshan Hot Spring Hotel, which had been funded and built by Fok Ying Tung, one of Hong Kong's most famous patriotic businessmen. On January 28, Deng Xiaoping met with Fok Ying Tung from Hong Kong and Ma Man-kei from Macao, as well as delegates from Macao's Nam Kwong (Group) Company Limited. With great confidence, Deng Xiaoping shared his thoughts on China's reform and opening-up, "It was my idea to set up the Special Economic Zones, and it was approved by the Central Committee. I am really glad to see that Zhongshan has chosen the right path, and is now developing very well." Fok Ying Tung agreed with excitement, "Indeed, we have very good policy." After sharing his thoughts on the reform and opening-up, Deng went on to talk about his expectations of Fok Ying Tung and Ma Man-kei in light of Hong Kong and Macao's return to China. Deng encouraged them to seize opportunities, carry on their cooperation with the central government, and make greater contributions to China's reform and opening-up.

欢聚一堂，谈笑风生。（自左至右：梁灵光、王震、霍英东、邓小平、马万祺、杨尚昆）

A cheerful gathering of old friends. (from left to right: Liang Lingguang, Wang Zhen, Fok Ying Tung, Deng Xiaoping, Ma Man-kei, Yang Shangkun)

壁画前。（左起：霍英东、邓小平、马万祺、杨尚昆）

In front of the mural. (from left: Fok Ying Tung, Deng Xiaoping, Ma Man-kei, Yang Shangkun)

赞赏中山市的旅游工作

在中山温泉宾馆中餐厅，看到墙壁上悬挂的极具岭南民俗风情的壁画，邓小平非常高兴，他对东道主霍英东说："你为中山市的旅游工作开了个好头！"

Praising the City of Zhongshan on Its Achievements in Tourism

At the restaurant of the Zhongshan Hot Spring Hotel, Deng Xiaoping happened to see a mural on the wall, which was full of distinctive Cantonese cultural elements. Deng was truly happy about what he saw, as he praised the host Fok Ying Tung, "Your work marks a really good start for the tourism industry in Zhongshan!"

“不走回头路”

中山温泉宾馆北面，罗三妹山旁边。

1 月 26 日晚餐后，邓小平很有闲情逸致，在傍山的小路上轻松散步。不料，外孙女绵绵扯了一根修长的茅草，顽皮地挡在小平面前，把茅草一横，娇声叫道：“不许过！”

邓小平不得不停下来，望着稚气未脱的外孙女，认真地说：“哎，爷爷是从来不走回头路的哟！”

邓楠清楚，老人家散步时是从来不肯走回头路的。她随即上前，冲女儿喊道：“快让开！”见母亲生气的样子，绵绵吐了吐舌头，做了个鬼脸，拿着茅草跑了。

看着这有趣的一幕，身边的人都笑了起来。

“Sticking to the Path”

In the evening of January 26, Deng Xiaoping took a leisurely stroll with his family outside the Zhongshan Hot Spring Hotel. Mianmian, Deng’s granddaughter, suddenly pulled a long grass branch and jokingly held it to block Deng’s way, “No trespassing!” Deng Xiaoping stopped and said to his lovely granddaughter in a serious tone, “You know, once the path is chosen, grandpa always sticks to it!” Deng Nan, Deng’s daughter, knew for a fact that Deng Xiaoping never changed his direction when taking a walk. She quickly stepped forward and yelled at her daughter, “Get out of the way!” Seeing her mother’s angry look, Mianmian stuck out her tongue and made a face, then ran off with the branch. This little incident cracked everyone up.

为珠海题词

1984 年 1 月 29 日上午，邓小平从中山返回珠海，在参观了珠海市容和狮山毛纺厂、电子厂后，在珠海宾馆听取了珠海市委书记、代市长的汇报。

午餐前，邓小平、杨尚昆、王震与澳门知名人士马万祺及珠海市的领导在宾馆的翠城餐厅休息，宾馆总经理在餐厅中间摆了笔墨纸砚，想请小平同志题词。小平同志朝桌子看了一眼，微微一笑，主动走到桌前，伏案挥毫，一口气题就："珠海经济特区好"。

见到小平同志的题词，珠海的同志喜出望外，这不是小平同志对珠海的轻易赞许，而是对珠海工作的充分肯定！

Writing an Inscription for Zhuhai

On January 29, 1984, Deng Xiaoping was briefed by the top party and government officials of Zhuhai at the Zhuhai Hotel, after paying a visit to the city's Shishan Woolen Factory and Electronics Factory.

Before lunch, Deng Xiaoping took a break with Yang Shangkun, Wang Zhen, Ma Man-kei and government officials of Zhuhai at the hotel's Cuicheng Dining Hall. The hotel's general manager had made the necessary preparation for Deng Xiaoping to write an inscription. Deng was glad to do so, as he wrote the following famous words for Zhuhai, "The Zhuhai Special Economic Zone has been a success."

The government officials of Zhuhai were truly overjoyed to see this, as they had realized that these words were not written casually, but actually filled with the highest approval from Deng Xiaoping on Zhuhai's development!

小平在珠岛宾馆散步

小平同志对深圳、蛇口、中山、珠海进行了将近六天的实地考察，1 月 29 日下午回到广州，下榻在珠岛宾馆一号楼。

经济特区欣欣向荣的景象，让小平同志感到无比欣慰，考察归来，他的脸上一直挂着笑容。在那充满岭南风情、如诗如画的珠岛宾馆，已是八十高龄的小平同志满身轻松，没有一点倦意，饭后稍事休息，走出月亮门，开始散步。工作人员劝他在房间休息，他说："散步就是最好的休息。"

Deng Xiaoping Taking a Walk at the Zhudao Guest House

After a six-day tour of Shenzhen, Shekou, Zhongshan and Zhuhai, Deng Xiaoping returned to Guangzhou on January 29 and stayed at the No.1 Building of the Zhudao Guest House.

Having seen the success and vitality of the Special Economic Zones himself, Deng Xiaoping felt happy and truly satisfied. At the age of eighty, he felt reinvigorated even after such a long and tiring trip. As he embarked on his usual evening walk after dinner, his staff advised him to take a break first. Deng replied, "Walking is the best relaxation."

接见珠岛宾馆工作人员

小平同志入住珠岛宾馆，让宾馆全体工作人员感到无比欣喜。他们在全力做好各项服务工作的同时，心里都有一个美好的愿望：若能同小平同志合一张影，该有多好！

小平同志的秘书把大家的愿望告诉了他，他非常痛快地答应了："好嘛好嘛，在哪儿照？"说完就快步走出房间，和时任广东省委第一书记任仲夷一起来到楼外。宾馆的服务员、保洁员、厨师等工作人员已经在楼前列好了队，见小平同志和仲夷书记满面笑容地走了过来，大家热烈地鼓起掌来。

Receiving the Staff of the Zhudao Guest House

The hotel staff were exhilarated about Deng Xiaoping staying at the Zhudao Guest House. As they provided the best services for Deng, they all shared a secret wish, that is, to take a photo with him.

After learning about the hotel staff's wish from his secretary, Deng Xiaoping did not hesitate to say yes, "Of course, where should we take the photo?" The hotel staff were so excited to see Deng Xiaoping come out and take photos with them that all of them started clapping their hands. In the end, Deng Xiaoping and Ren Zhongyi, party chief of Guangdong, took a picture with everyone from the hotel.

视察白天鹅宾馆

坐落在广州市珠江水面上的白天鹅宾馆，是香港知名企业家霍英东、彭国珍与广东省人民政府合资兴建的中国第一家五星级酒店。

改革开放之前，处于祖国南大门的广州市，没有一家像样的宾馆酒店承办每年两届的广交会，来宾的接待都成了大问题。改革开放初期，广东省委冲破条条框框的束缚，率先与港商合作，合资建起了这座大型的现代化酒店。白天鹅宾馆为广东的开放搭建了一座漂亮的平台，吸引了若干外商和大量外资。

白天鹅宾馆建成开业后，很多海外企业家、外国政要纷纷前来入住，20 世纪 80 年代，邓小平曾三次莅临白天鹅宾馆。1984 年 1 月，小平同志首次来到为特区改革开放做出很大贡献的白天鹅宾馆，宾馆的全体员工拿出最大的热情迎接这位给祖国带来新生的伟人。

宾馆的西餐厅制作的法国面包，勾起了小平同志青年时代在法国勤工俭学的回忆，他每次来都要品尝，还特别提出要吃“硬的法国面包”。1985 年他来白天鹅宾馆，临走时还掏钱买了几个给孩子们带回去。

在宾馆领导的陪同下，小平同志仔细参观了白天鹅宾馆，他站在宾馆高层的走廊里，隔着咖啡色的玻璃窗眺望面前的珠江，对陪同的同志说：“不栽梧桐树，怎能引得凤凰来？白天鹅就是我们国家的第一棵梧桐树嘛！看来我们还要再开放一些城市。”

果然，小平同志回京后不久，国家就宣布再开放 14 个沿海城市。

Inspecting the White Swan Hotel

Located on Shamian Island and overlooking the Pearl River, the White Swan Hotel in Guangzhou was China's first five-star hotel. It was funded and built by Hong Kong businessmen Fok Ying Tung and Pang Kwok-chan in collaboration with the Guangdong Provincial People's Government.

At the heart of southern China, Guangzhou was seriously lacking nice hotels that could accommodate guests from home and abroad during the famous Canton Fair that was held twice a year. The problem had lasted until the beginning of China's reform and opening-up, when the CPC Guangdong Provincial Committee broke the old rules and took the lead in working with Hong Kong businessmen to build joint venture hotels like the White Swan. As it turned out, the White Swan Hotel became an international platform for the opening-up of Guangdong, attracting numerous foreign investors and investment every year.

Since its opening, the White Swan Hotel had received countless foreign leaders and entrepreneurs, while Deng Xiaoping himself visited the hotel three times in the 1980s. In January 1984, Deng came to the hotel for the first time, in recognition of the great contributions it had made to China's reform and opening-up. The entire hotel staff had welcomed and served the architect of modern China with the greatest enthusiasm.

Deng Xiaoping was particularly fond of the French baguette made by the hotel's chefs, because it brought back memories when he work-studied in France as a youngster. He would always have a taste of the baguette, what he called"hard French bread", every time he visited the hotel. During his 1985 visit to the White Swan, he even bought a few pieces of baguette to take home for his grandchildren.

During his tour of the White Swan Hotel, he stood in the corridor of the hotel's top floor and looked out on the Pearl River through the tainted glass windows, saying,"How can you attract phoenix without planting the Chinese parasol tree? I think the White Swan Hotel is our country's first phoenix tree to attract foreign investors and investment! It looks like we have to open up more cities."

Sure enough, China announced the opening of another fourteen coastal cities to overseas investment shortly after Deng Xiaoping returned to Beijing.

军区欢迎晚会

为欢迎小平同志来南方视察，广州军区在军区礼堂专门组织了一台文艺晚会，热烈欢迎共和国军队的最高统帅。

1984 年 1 月 30 日晚，小平同志来到广州军区礼堂，欣赏部队文艺工作者的精彩演出。演职员们用艺术的语言，展示出改革开放大潮席卷南粤大地的恢弘场景，讴歌了改革开放的英明决策。欢歌、笑语、掌声在演出现场融汇，将党心、民心、军心紧密地凝聚在一起。

演出结束后，小平同志走上舞台。此时，台上台下掌声雷动，演员和观众都为目睹改革开放总设计师的风采而发出阵阵欢呼。

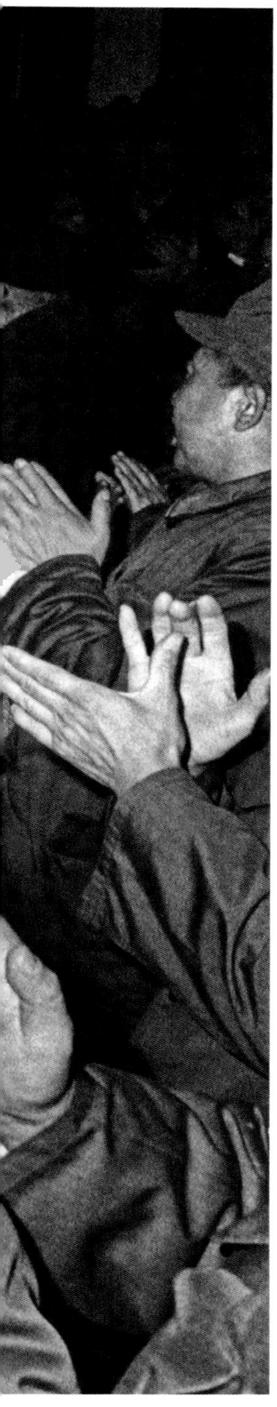

Welcome Party at the Guangzhou Military Region

The Guangzhou Military Region had prepared an evening gala in its auditorium to express their warmest welcome to Deng Xiaoping's visit as the country's commander-in-chief.

In the evening of January 30, 1984, Deng Xiaoping came to the auditorium of the Guangzhou Military Region to enjoy the wonderful performances by the military's artists. Using the language of art, the performers demonstrated the magnificent scenes in the reform and opening-up of southern China, and expressed their appreciation and support for the wisdom of the reform program. The gala was a big success and further united the party, the people and the military.

After the show was over, Deng Xiaoping walked on stage to express his appreciation for the wonderful performance. Both the performers and the audience gave him a standing ovation, because it was truly a precious opportunity for them to meet the architect of China's reform and opening-up in person.

视察北京市政建设

1990 年 4 月 29 日，邓小平在时任北京市副市长张百发的陪同下视察北京新建居民区。20 世纪 50 年代，张百发曾作为突击队长参与建设人民大会堂。1981 年，他出任北京市副市长，主管城建。邓小平先视察了北京蒲黄榆、双榆树地区的住宅小区，之后查看了三元桥、机场路、亚运村等地。每查看一地，邓小平都会提出一些带有前瞻性的细节问题，让大家耳目一新，深受启发。当时，北京正处于筹办 1990 年第 11 届亚运会期间，当年的大量的城市住宅和市政建设为今天北京的城市发展格局奠定了基础。在视察过程中，我与小平同志同乘一辆车。拍摄时，为了能够展现城市建设的场景，我使用了当时德国进口的摇头机进行拍摄，将人物与北京的建设场景糅合在一个画面之中。

Inspecting Urban Construction in Beijing

On April 29, 1990, Deng Xiaoping inspected the building of new residential areas in Beijing. Accompanying him on the tour was the city's vice mayor Zhang Baifa, who had participated in the construction of the Great Hall of the People in the 1950s. In 1981, he was appointed the vice mayor of Beijing and was put in charge of urban development. During the tour, Deng Xiaoping inspected some of the major construction projects at the time, including residential neighborhoods and the Asian Games Village. He would raise detailed, forward-looking questions for each place he had visited. A great deal of urban housing and city construction had been done during Beijing's preparation for the 11th Asian Games in 1990, which actually laid the foundation for the pattern of the city's urban planning today. I rode in the same car with Deng Xiaoping during his inspection. To capture meaningful moments that would tell stories behind the city's construction, I specifically used the German-made panoramic camera to take pictures that day, so that I was able to blend my subjects with the scenes in a single image.

小平同志关注上海

1991 年 2 月 18 日，农历大年初四的上午，邓小平兴致勃勃地登上了上海新锦江大酒店 41 层的旋转餐厅，一边透过宽敞明亮的玻璃窗眺望上海中心城区的面貌，一边嘱咐身旁的朱镕基：“我们说上海开发晚了，要努力干啊！”

Deng Xiaoping's Expectations of Shanghai

It was the morning of the fourth day of the Lunar New Year, February 18, 1991. With great excitement, Deng Xiaoping visited the observatory revolving restaurant of the Jin Jiang Tower, located on the 41st floor. As he looked out on the cityscape of downtown Shanghai through the bright glass windows, he told Zhu Rongji, then mayor of Shanghai, "Now we know the development of Shanghai is a bit late in the game, we really have to work hard!"

新锦江大酒店的旋转餐厅里挂着两幅大地图，一幅是上海地图，另一幅是浦东新区地图，地图旁摆着浦东开发的模型，就像当年组织重大战役备战时的情景一样。邓小平看着地图和模型，说："抓紧浦东开发，不要动摇，一直到建成。只要守信用，按照国际惯例办事，人家首先会把资金投到上海，竞争就要靠这个竞争。"

Two large maps were put up in the revolving restaurant of the Jin Jiang Tower. One was a map of Shanghai, and the other was a map of the Pudong New Area. With maps and models displaying the city's development, it looked like a war room in the revolutionary days. Keeping his eyes on the maps and models, Deng Xiaoping made an important remark, "We must stick to the path of development for Pudong, without any oscillation, until its completion. We must also keep our promises and act in accordance with international practice. We need foreign investments to come to Shanghai first, and we'll build up our strength from here."

视察南浦大桥施工现场。（左一为杨尚昆，左二为朱镕基）

Inspecting the construction site of the Nanpu Bridge. (first from left, Yang Shangkun; second from left, Zhu Rongji)

小平同志视察建设中的南浦大桥

小平同志一直关心上海浦东开发区的建设，曾于 1991 年、1992 年、1993 年三次亲临南浦大桥、杨浦大桥施工现场视察。

1991 年 2 月 18 日，农历正月初四，小平同志第一次来到南浦大桥施工工地。他和一同前来视察的杨尚昆主席仰着头、挥着手，向节假日仍然战斗在施工前线的建筑工人们拜年问好，在几十米高的桥墩上施工的工人们也一起给两位老革命家拜年。小平同志非常想过江到浦东看看，可是大桥的建造位置正处于码头的摆渡口，船只无法通行，只能站在南码头的浮桥上看一下，由建桥工程总指挥朱志豪将大桥什么时候开工、什么时候完工、投资多少、工程进度等情况向他做了汇报。

Inspecting the Nanpu Bridge under Construction

Deng Xiaoping had always concerned himself with the development of the Pudong Development Zone in Shanghai, visiting the construction sites of the Nanpu Bridge and Yangpu Bridge three times in 1991, 1992 and 1993.

On February 18, 1991, the fourth day of the Lunar New Year, Deng Xiaoping visited the construction site of the Nanpu Bridge for the first time, with Yang Shangkun, then President of China. The two seasoned revolutionaries raised their heads and waved at the construction workers, who were working on the bridge tiers of several dozen meters high. As Deng and Yang paid their respect to the workers who put work first even during China's traditional holiday, the workers also greeted them with excitement from above. Deng Xiaoping would very much want to cross the river and visit Pudong for himself. However, because of some technical difficulties, it was impossible to do so at the time. As a compromise, Deng could only stand on the floating landing stage and take a look from afar, while listening to detailed reports about the progress of the bridge's construction given by Zhu Zhihao, the bridge project manager.

开发浦东的蓝图，早就在小平同志心中了。他对时任上海市委书记兼市长的朱镕基说：“那一年确定四个经济特区，主要是从地理条件考虑的……没有考虑到上海在人才方面的优势。上海人聪明，素质好，如果当时就确定在上海也设经济特区，现在就不是这个样子……开发浦东，这个影响就大了，不只是浦东的问题，是关系上海发展的问题，是利用上海这个基地发展长江三角洲和长江流域的问题。”不过，邓小平用他一贯的自信和乐观做了总结：“这是件坏事，但也是好事，你们可以借鉴经验，可以搞得好一点，后来居上。”

从南浦大桥施工现场出来，邓小平兴致勃勃地来到新锦江大酒店 41 层的旋转餐厅，朱镕基向邓小平汇报了浦东开发开放中“金融先行”的一些打算和做法。邓小平听完后说：“金融很重要，是现代经济的核心。金融搞好了，一着棋活，全盘皆活。上海过去是金融中心，是货币自由兑换的地方，今后也要这样搞。中国在金融方面取得国际地位，首先要靠上海。那要好多年以后，但现在就要做起。”“要克服一个怕字，要有勇气。”“什么事情总要有人试第一个，才能开拓新路。试第一个就要准备失败，失败也不要紧。希望上海人民思想更解放一点，胆子更大一点，步子更快一点。”

The development of Pudong had long been part of Deng Xiaoping's larger plan. He once told Zhu Rongji, then the mayor and party chief of Shanghai, "Setting up the first four Special Economic Zones were mainly out of geographical consideration, while we did not consider much the advantages of Shanghai in terms of its talents. The people of Shanghai are known to be smart and capable. If the city had been made one of the first special economic zones, we wouldn't have the problems today. … The development of Pudong will certainly have a much bigger impact, which should be related to the development of Shanghai as a whole. It is actually about taking advantage of Shanghai as a base for the overall development of the Yangtze River Delta and the Yangtze River Basin." Confident and optimistic as always, Deng Xiaoping added, "It's just like every coin has two sides. While Shanghai is somewhat late in the game, it can learn from previous experience, achieve greater success, and catch up much faster."

Leaving the construction site of the Nanpu Bridge, Deng Xiaoping arrived at the revolving restaurant located on the 41st floor of the Jin Jiang Tower, where Zhu Rongji briefed him about the Shanghai government's strategy of emphasizing the role of finance in the development and opening-up of Pudong. Deng was very happy to hear this, "Finance is very important, it is the core of modern economy. It is a good idea to put more emphasis on finance, it is a smart chess move that will help us win the whole game. Shanghai used to be the national center of finance, where there was a free exchange of currency. We should do the same thing in future. The international status of China in terms of finance depends first and foremost on the success of Shanghai. While it may take years to accomplish our goals, we must start right away." Deng went on to encourage Zhu Rongji and the people of Shanghai, saying, "It is important to be brave, and to overcome the fear of failure." "There is always a first time, and to be a trailblazer, you have to be prepared for defeats. It's OK if you fail. I wish the people of Shanghai can become more liberated in their mind, and take bolder and faster steps in the reform."

向南浦大桥施工现场的工人挥手致意。（右一为黄菊，右二为吴邦国）

Waving to the workers at the construction site of the Nanpu Bridge. (first from right, Huang Ju; second from right, Wu Bangguo)

视察建成的南浦大桥。（左一为倪天增，左二为吴邦国）
Inspecting the completed Nanpu Bridge. (first from left, Ni Tianzeng; second from left, Wu Bangguo)

在南浦大桥上的珍贵合影

邓小平同志亲笔题字的南浦大桥横跨南北，打通了黄浦江两岸的发展经脉。他对上海的感情由来已久，在深圳先行一步之后，老人把目光投向了这个曾经的国际大都市。

1992 年 2 月 7 日，农历正月初四，邓小平、杨尚昆一行来到已经正式通车的南浦大桥。老人下车后，仰望大桥雄姿，由衷地赞叹说：“南浦大桥具有国际领先水平。”他又指着大桥横梁上镶着的“南浦大桥”四个大字，拉着卓琳说：“大桥为国家争了光，我的题字也没有给大桥丢丑。”说完，他和卓琳开心地拍了一张合影。

A Precious Photo on the Nanpu Bridge

One of the main bridges in Shanghai, the Nanpu Bridge connects the west of the Huangpu River with the east of Huangpu. Deng Xiaoping personally inscribed the name of the bridge on its main girder. Given his long-standing affections for Shanghai, Deng began to pay more attention to its role in China's reform and opening-up after his initial emphasis on Shenzhen.

On February 7, 1992, the fourth day of the Lunar New Year, Deng Xiaoping and Yang Shangkun paid a visit to the Nanpu Bridge, which had been officially opened for public use. Looking at the bridge's magnificent structure, Deng praised its success with heartfelt admiration, "The Nanpu Bridge has truly achieved top international standards." Pointing to his inscription of the bridge's name on the main girder, he said to his wife Zhuo Lin, "The bridge has brought great honor to our country, and my inscription is now part of its glory." The couple then took a photo together on the bridge.

视察黄浦江两岸

1991 年 2 月 18 日，小平同志在杨尚昆、朱镕基及家人的陪同下，沿着黄浦江西岸视察。望着南浦大桥热火朝天的施工场面，听到江对岸传来的推土机、挖掘机、起重机的阵阵轰鸣声，小平同志仿佛看到了深圳特区当年的建设场景。浦东这个更新更大的经济特区正拔地而起，总设计师心中的蓝图即将变成现实，想到这里，小平同志情不自禁地露出开心的笑容。

A Tour of the Huangpu River

On February 18, 1991, Deng Xiaoping inspected the west bank of the Huangpu River, accompanied by Yang Shangkun, Zhu Rongji and his family. The construction scenes of the Nanpu Bridge, as well as the roaring sounds of the bulldozers, excavators and cranes, reminded him of the development of the Shenzhen Special Economic Zone a few years ago. With the rise of Pudong as a much bigger and more advanced economic zone, the blueprint of China's reform and opening-up was becoming reality. Thinking about this, Deng could not help but smile.

在旗忠村

1992 年 2 月 12 日，邓小平在上海闵行开发区视察完毕，又来到上海县马桥乡旗忠村视察。旗忠村小学门口，锣鼓喧天，小学生们跳起舞，打起鼓，高声喊着："邓爷爷好！"小平同志格外高兴。这时，一个大约两三岁的小孩，挣开母亲的双手，摇摇晃晃地向小平同志这个方向走来。一下子，人们的目光都集中在这个孩子的身上。这时，不知谁喊了一句"让邓爷爷亲亲"，吴邦国同志马上过去抱起孩子，小平同志高兴地在孩子的小脸蛋上亲了亲。那慈祥和蔼的样子，就跟在家里亲自己小孙子时一模一样。

At the Qizhong Village

After finishing his tour of the Minhang Development Zone in Shanghai, Deng Xiaoping paid a visit to Qizhong Village in Maqiao Town of Shanghai County. Students from the Qizhong Village Primary School had gathered together to welcome Deng's visit, cheering and shouting "Hello, Grandpa Deng!" Amid all the excitement, a two-year-old toddler broke away from his mother and wobbled his way towards Deng. While all eyes were focused on this child, someone suddenly shouted, "Let Grandpa Deng give the baby a kiss." Upon hearing this, Wu Bangguo immediately went over to pick up the child and handed him over to Deng Xiaoping. Feeling truly happy, Deng kissed the child on his cheek. The way Deng Xiaoping had kissed the child was filled with the same love and affection like when he kissed his own grandchildren at home.

吴邦国（左一）向邓小平介绍电子元件。
Wu Bangguo (first from left) showing some electronic components to Deng Xiaoping.

参观贝岭

1992 年 2 月 10 日的上海，虽然天气晴朗，但春寒料峭。邓小平一行来到了地处上海西南的漕河泾工业开发区，视察生产电子元件的上海贝岭微电子公司。公司的 300 多位中外员工非常兴奋，因为此前他们已经得到邓小平要来的消息。这消息就像春风，吹遍了贝岭公司的每一个角落。

厂方决定安排贵宾参观硅片制造部。接待人员把邓小平一行引到一批先进生产设备和大束流离子注入机旁，介绍说："这是经过国际巴统会特批首次进入我国的。"听到这里，邓小平若有所思地询问技术人员："这些设备是姓'资'还是姓'社'？"吴邦国率先回答："姓'社'。资本主义国家的设备拿来为我们社会主义所用，那就是姓'社'了。"

邓小平来到院子里，一批热情活泼的员工涌上来把小平团团围住。小平一点也不拘束，亲切地和大家握手。大家按捺不住内心的喜悦，纷纷向小平挥手，表达祝愿小平同志健康长寿的美意。这时候，小平同志特意靠近他女儿邓榕的手持录音机，语重心长地回应道："下个世纪靠你们！"在场的所有人深切地领会到老人家对他们的殷切期望。

Visiting the Shanghai Belling Micro-electronics Manufacturing Company

The weather was still chilly in early Spring in Shanghai. On February 10, 1992, Deng Xiaoping paid a visit to the Shanghai Belling Micro-electronics Manufacturing Company located in Shanghai's Caohejing Industrial Park. More than 300 Chinese and foreign employees of the company were genuinely excited about Deng's visit. The news was like a spring breeze, warming up the heart of everyone in the company.

As the company's VIP, Deng Xiaoping was given a special tour of the manufacturing department of the silicon wafer, where he was shown the most advanced equipment that the company had. When Deng Xiaoping learned that these instruments had been exported to China with the special approval of the Coordinating Committee for Multilateral Export Controls, he raised a thoughtful question for the technician, "Are the equipment elements of capitalism or socialism?"

Wu Bangguo answered first, "Of course, they are socialist ones. When the equipment from capitalist countries are used for socialist purposes, they become elements of socialism." As Deng Xiaoping walked to the courtyard, he was immediately surrounded by a group of enthusiastic employees. Feeling at ease, Deng shook hands with everyone cordially. The workers could not hold back their joy and excitement, as they waved to Deng and expressed their best wishes for him. At this moment, Deng Xiaoping purposefully approached the hand-held recorder that his daughter Deng Rong was holding, and announced his most heartfelt thoughts, "The future of China in the next century depends on you!" Everyone present felt and understood Deng Xiaoping's ardent expectations of them.

邓小平对在场的中外技术人员语重心长地说："下个世纪靠你们！"

Deng Xiaoping shared his most heartfelt wishes with the technicians in attendance, saying to them, "The future of China in the next century depends on you!"

视察上海航天局

1992 年 2 月 13 日，邓小平、杨尚昆一行来到位于闵行的上海航天局运载火箭总装厂，这是小平同志第二次亲临上海航天基地视察。

老人家一边听着专家对航天产品的介绍，一边饶有兴致地发问。当得知我国运载火箭 20 多年来连续发射均告成功时，他称赞道："你们办得好，我们这个队伍独一无二，几十年的锻炼，你们没有失败过。"此时，上海航天局局长苏世表示："中国航天事业的发展，都是在党中央，在老一代无产阶级革命家开创下才发展起来的。"邓小平却对他说："决策靠我们，我们是政治决策，但是把它干出来，还是靠你们。感谢航天人为改革开放做出的贡献，中国也要在世界高科技领域占一席之地。"

Visiting the Shanghai Academy of Spaceflight Technology

On February 13, 1992, Deng Xiaoping and Yang Shangkun visited the launch vehicle assembly plant of the Shanghai Academy of Spaceflight Technology in Minhang District. This was the second time Deng had visited the Shanghai space base in person.

Deng Xiaoping listened to the experts' introduction of space technology with great interest and asked many questions. When he learned that China's launch vehicles had enjoyed a streak of successful launches for more than twenty years, he was truly happy, "You have done a wonderful job, and you have a unique team. You have never failed during decades of practice." At this point, Su Shi, director of the Shanghai Academy of Spaceflight Technology, said, "The development of China's space industry has been successful because it has always been under the leadership of the CPC Central Committee, and has always been supported by the old generation of proletarian revolutionaries." However, Deng Xiaoping disagreed, "We make the decisions, that is our responsibility as politicians, but it is still up to all of you to get the work done. We must thank everyone who works hard for China's space development. Without their contribution, it is impossible for China to develop its own high technology and take its place in this world."

邓小平在运载火箭总装厂。（右一为杨尚昆，右二为朱镕基）

Deng Xiaoping at the launch vehicle assembly plant. (first from right, Yang Shangkun; second from right, Zhu Rongji)

参观仙湖植物园

始建于 1983 年的仙湖植物园，位于深圳市罗湖区东郊的莲塘仙湖路。1992 年 1 月 22 日，第二次到深圳视察的邓小平来到这里。

阳光灿烂，春风和煦，公园里绿树婆娑，鲜花盛开，袭来阵阵芬芳。小平同志先在大厅里观看了植物园的模型沙盘，听了工作人员对植物园和珍稀植物的简单介绍，而后在国家主席杨尚昆及省、市领导的陪同下，进入植物园参观。

这个植物园的面积并不大，却种养了来自全国的 8000 多种植物，其中珍稀植物就有 100 余种。几种名称很有意思的树种引起邓小平和家人的浓厚兴趣，如“发财树”“光棍树”“天鹅绒竹芋”“跳舞兰”“湘妃竹”等等。当园艺师告诉小平“这些湘妃竹就是从您的老家四川成都移植过来的”，邓小平打趣地说：“这有个产权问题啊！”大家听了都笑了起来。

在这宛如仙境的植物园里游览参观，小平同志格外轻松，时不时地开几句玩笑。我脖子上挂了几部照相机，忙着为小平同志拍照。趁小平停住脚步的空隙，我走上前去向他握手问好：“邓伯伯好！”他的小女儿毛毛（邓榕）告诉他：“小二哥可是大摄影家，他是中国摄影家协会的副主席哩！”小平同志看了看头上汗津津的我，笑着说：“好哇，你们杨家出了两个主席呢！”说完跟着大家一起笑了起来，我的父亲、国家主席杨尚昆也同样忍不住哈哈大笑。

离开前，小平同志和杨尚昆主席在植物园各植下一棵高山榕。

A Trip to the Fairy Lake Botanical Garden

Founded in 1983, the Fairy Lake Botanical Garden is located at the foot of Wutong Mountain, beside the Shenzhen Reservoir in Shenzhen's Luohu District. On January 22, 1992, Deng Xiaoping paid a visit to the garden during his second tour of Shenzhen.

It was a warm, sunny day in spring, and flowers were in full bloom everywhere. Deng Xiaoping first inspected the model sand table of the botanical garden in the great hall, where he was given a brief introduction about the rare plants in the garden. He then entered the garden for a tour, accompanied by President Yang Shangkun and top officials of Guangdong and Shenzhen.

The garden was home to more than 8,000 species of plants from around China, including more than 100 species of rare plants. Deng Xiaoping and his family were attracted by several special species with interesting Chinese nicknames, such as the "Fortune Tree", the "Bachelor Tree", the "Velvet Bamboo Taro", the "dancing orchids", the "Xiangfei Zhu" (spotted bamboo) and so on. When the horticulturist told Deng that the spotted bamboo was actually transplanted from Deng's hometown of Sichuan, Deng Xiaoping jokingly said, "Looks like we have a property rights issue at hand!" People burst into laugher when they heard this.

Taking a tour in this fairyland-like botanical garden, Deng Xiaoping was unusually relaxed, as he told jokes now and then. As I followed him closely with several cameras hanging around my neck, I was busy taking photos. At one point, when he stopped for a rest, I walked up and shook hands with him, saying, "Hello, Uncle Deng!" Maomao, Deng's youngest daughter, told his father: "Brother Xiao Er (my nickname) is not only a great photographer now, he is also the vice president of the Chinese Photographers Association!" Deng Xiaoping smiled and commented, "Well, now you have two presidents in the Yang family!" Everyone started laughing, and Yang Shangkun, my father and then President of China, couldn't help laughing too.

At the end of their tour, Deng Xiaoping and President Yang Shangkun each planted an alpine banyan in the garden.

阳光灿烂，春风和煦，小平同志和家人一起参观仙湖植物园。
Deng Xiaoping and his family visited the Fairy Lake Botanical Garden on a sunny spring day.

XCITY

敬爱的小平

1992 年，春寒料峭，邓小平和卓琳在上海西郊宾馆欢度春节。

邓小平与上海有着特殊的情缘。1920 年，赴法国勤工俭学，16 岁的邓小平就是从黄浦江畔登船出发的。1949 年 5 月初，时任总前委书记的邓小平，部署了解放上海的战役；5 月 27 日，上海获得解放。中华人民共和国成立以后，邓小平曾几十次来上海。邓小平对上海有着深深的眷恋，他晚年连续七年在上海和上海人民共度春节。他多次谆谆嘱咐上海市党政领导：“抓紧浦东开发，不要动摇，一直到建成。”

在上海的 18 天里，邓小平反复强调了一个观点：发展才是硬道理。他说，上海民心比较顺，这是一股无穷的力量。目前完全有条件上得更快一点，上海改革开放胆子要更大一点，看准了就要大胆地试，大胆地闯。

1984 年，是改革开放的总设计师邓小平同志首次去南方视察，作出“建立经济特区的政策是正确的”这一判断，为我国进一步改革开放奠定了时代的最强音，为建设中国特色的社会主义指明了道路。1992 年邓小平第二次去南方视察，发表了南方谈话，极大地推动了中国改革开放的进程。对中国 90 年代的经济改革与社会进步起到了关键的推动作用，对 21 世纪中国的改革与发展，仍将产生深远的影响。

Hello Xiaoping!

Deng Xiaoping and Zhuo Lin celebrated the Lunar New Year at the Xijiao State Guest Hotel in the chilly spring of 1992. Throughout his life, Deng had developed a special bond with Shanghai. When he travelled by ship to France to participate in the Diligent Work-Frugal Study Movement at the tender age of 16, he actually embarked from the banks of the Huangpu River. In early May 1949, Deng Xiaoping, then secretary of the general front committee, deployed the campaign to liberate Shanghai, which was liberated on May 27. After the founding of the People's Republic of China, Deng Xiaoping visited Shanghai dozens of times. Therefore, he had held deep and longstanding affections for Shanghai, and this explained why, in his retirement, he had spent the Spring Festival with the people of Shanghai for seven consecutive years. He had instructed the party and government leaders of Shanghai on multiple occasions about the importance of Pudong's development, "It is important to pay more attention to the development of Pudong, and we cannot let up our efforts until its successful completion."

During his 18-day stay in Shanghai this time, Deng Xiaoping had repeatedly emphasized one point: development is of overriding importance. As far as Deng was concerned, the support from the people of Shanghai had provided enduring strength for the city's reform and opening-up. Given the favorable conditions, he believed it was absolutely necessary for Shanghai to take bigger and bolder steps in its reform and opening-up. "Once we are sure that something should be done, we should dare to experiment and break a new path."

As the chief architect of China's reform and opening-up, Deng Xiaoping embarked on his first southern tour in 1984. On that trip, he confirmed the country's commitment to the reform program by pointing out, "The development and experience of Shenzhen have proved the correctness of our policy on the establishment of Special Economic Zones". Without doubt, Deng's first southern tour had sounded the strongest notes for China's further reform and opening-up, while also clearly pointing out the direction for building socialism with Chinese characteristics. In 1992, Deng Xiaoping made his second southern tour and delivered the famous southern talks during the trip, which had greatly promoted the cause of China's reform and opening-up. Deng's second southern tour has not only played a key role in promoting China's economic reform and social progress in the 1990s, but will also continue to have a profound impact on the reform and development of China in the 21st century.

平凡生活

AN ORDINARY MAN

"邓家添丁，'82+1'，真逗！"

"A new member added to the Deng family, 82+1, how interesting!"

邓小平是一位举世公认的伟人，也是一位感情充沛、兴趣广泛的普通人。他很喜欢散步、登山、游泳、打桥牌、练书法、阅读武侠小说。在家里，忙完了手上的工作，他便和孙辈们嬉戏玩耍，孩子们也都喜欢黏在爷爷身边。

然而，这些兴趣爱好和生活乐趣，直到他退休之后才有了时间尽情享受。为了弥补亲情上的缺憾，每次外出，他都尽可能带上全家人，共享天伦之乐。他尊敬一直与全家人相依为命的继母，他关爱满堂的儿孙，他是一位有血有肉、有情有义的慈祥老人。

In addition to being an extraordinary leader, Deng Xiaoping was also an ordinary man with feelings like everyone else. He had many interests, such as walking, hiking, swimming, playing bridge, practicing Chinese calligraphy as well as reading martial arts novels. After finishing the work at hand, he would play with his grandchildren and become their favorite grandfather.

However, Deng Xiaoping didn't have the time for all these interests and hobbies until his retirement. To make up for past regrets, he would take his entire family with him whenever he had to go on a trip, so that he could spend more time with his loved ones. He had utmost respect for his stepmother who had been with the Deng family through thick and thin, and he truly loved his children and grandchildren. As far as his family was concerned, he was just an ordinary old man with the most common affections.

在北戴河过生日

（一）

1989 年 8 月 22 日，邓小平迎来了 85 岁生日。为了照相，老人家特意穿上了许久不穿的中山装。为了拍好小平同志的生日纪念照，我把拍摄地点选择在浴场边上的观景平台。老人家神清气爽地站在观景阳台上，眺望大海，目光深邃。

Birthday Celebrations in Beidaihe

August 22, 1989 marked the 85th birthday of Deng Xiaoping. In order to pose for his birthday photo, Deng put on a Mao suit that he hadn't worn in quite a while. Hoping to get the best picture, I had decided to take the photo at the observation deck of the beach resort. Looking invigorated on the platform, Deng Xiaoping took a long and deep gaze at the sea.

（二）

1984 年 8 月 22 日傍晚，不少中央领导同志都兴致勃勃地赶来出席为邓小平八十寿辰举行的晚餐会。

小平同志神采奕奕，精神焕发，同前来贺寿的胡耀邦同志亲切握手。

In the evening of August 22, 1984, many leaders of the CPC Central Committee had attended Deng Xiaoping's 80th birthday party with great excitement. Looking energetic and in great spirits, Deng shook hands warmly with Hu Yaobang, who had come to send his best wishes.

（三）

1984 年 8 月 22 日晚，邓小平在北戴河和家人共度八十寿辰。为了表达对邓小平同志的敬重和爱戴，北京饭店的专业糕点师精心设计制作了一个十层大蛋糕，并点缀着 80 颗具有民族传统特色的大寿桃，中西合璧的鲜明风格，让大家眼前一亮。

邓小平邀请在场的天真活泼的孩子们和他一起鼓起腮帮吹蜡烛，餐厅里欢乐的气氛达到了高潮。这张照片后来由新华社向国内外发稿，吸引了众多国内外读者。

Deng Xiaoping celebrated his 80th birthday with his family in Beidaihe on August 22, 1984. In order to express their heartfelt respect for Deng Xiaoping, the pastry chefs from Beijing Hotel had prepared a ten-layer cake for the occasion, which was decorated with eighty longevity peaches with traditional Chinese characteristics. Combining both elements from Chinese and Western cultures, the cake turned out to be a big hit at the party.

The joy of the party reached its climax when Deng Xiaoping invited the lovely children to blow out the candles with him. This photo was later picked up by Xinhua News Agency and released to the world, which attracted the attention of numerous audiences at home and abroad.

退下来以后的邓小平

这组表现邓小平安享退休生活的系列照片，获得了 1988 年第 31 届世界新闻摄影大赛中人物组照的“金眼奖”。一方面，这与中国领导人日益增强的国际影响力分不开；另一方面，这展现了退休后的中国领导人真实而自然的一面——邓小平一向的愿望是有步骤地退下，真正过一个平凡人的生活。

小平同志从领导岗位退下来后，愈发引起社会各界的关注，人们非常渴望了解小平同志的退休生活。对我来说，小平同志退休后，我和他老人家接触的机会有增无减。

1987 年冬天的一天，在院子里披着大衣散步的邓小平和小孙子相遇。爷孙俩双双张开双臂迎向对方的瞬间，被我及时抓住。这富有戏剧性的一幕，展现了血浓于水的人间亲情。

Deng Xiaoping in His Retirement

Focusing on Deng Xiaoping's life in retirement, this group of photos won the 3rd prize in the"People in the News" category in the 31st World Press Photo Contest held in 1988. While the award-winning photos certainly testified to the rising international influence of Chinese leaders, they also received international acclaim for telling the true stories about the retired Chinese leader Deng Xiaoping. It had always been Deng's wish to step down from his various leadership positions and lead an ordinary life.

People from all walks of life in China became increasingly intrigued by Deng Xiaoping's life in retirement. Luckily for me, my chances of coming into contact with him had actually increased since his retirement.

This photo was taken in the winter of 1987. While walking in the courtyard with an overcoat draped over his shoulders, Deng Xiaoping run into his grandson. I captured the moment when both the grandpa and the grandson opened their arms to embrace each other. The photo therefore preserved a moment of true affection between Deng Xiaoping and his family.

读金庸武侠小说

金庸，本名查良镛，浙江海宁人，被誉为“香港四大才子”之一。他是著名爱国人士，又是当代武侠小说作家、著名报人，曾荣获剑桥大学博士学位。

邓小平以读书为毕生乐趣，读马列著作，博览中外经典，乐此不疲。他对书籍的阅读面很广，就连武侠小说他也常常看。1981 年，邓小平接见金庸时，第一句话就是：“欢迎查先生回来看看，你的小说我读过。我们已经是老朋友了。”

Reading Martial Arts Novels by Jin Yong

Born in Haining, Zhejiang and better known by his pen name Jin Yong, Cha Leung-yung was arguably the most famous wuxia (martial arts) novelist in contemporary China. Lauded one of the "Four Talents in Hong Kong", he co-founded *Ming Pao*, an influential Hong Kong daily newspaper, and served as its chief editor. Holding a doctorate from Cambridge University, he was especially known for his love and patriotism for his motherland, China.

Reading was a lifelong passion for Deng Xiaoping. He had a long reading list that was not limited to the works of Marx and Lenin or the world's classics, and he often dipped into martial arts novels for fun. The first thing that Deng Xiaoping said to Jin Yong when they met for the first time in 1981 was, "Welcome back, Mr. Cha. I have read all your novels, and I feel like we are already old friends."

看孙

1985 年，邓小平的嫡孙邓卓棣降生，刚满月就被父母送回了北京，这是邓家的一件大事。

8 月的一天，在北戴河，爷爷终于有机会尽情地看一看小爱孙。邓小平坐在藤椅上，侧过身子，轻轻掀起摇篮的顶盖，深情地端详在襁褓中熟睡的小家伙。爷爷的动作很轻、很慢，眼神里饱含着爱意，生怕打搅了小孙子的甜梦。这个看似平凡的情景，在饱经风霜的老人家那里，却有着丰富而凝重的内涵。老人家凝望良久，思绪万千。女儿邓榕一直蹲在父亲身后，陪着老人家一起分享这一刻的感动。

Checking on His Grandson

The Deng family welcomed a new member with the birth of Deng Xiaoping's grandchild, Deng Zhuodi in 1985. Zhuodi was only one month old when he was brought back to Beijing by his parents to reunite with Deng Xiaoping.

This photo was taken in Beidaihe in August 1985, when Deng Xiaoping finally got the opportunity to look after his dear grandson. Sitting on a rattan armchair and turning sideways, Deng Xiaoping gently lifted the top cover of the cradle, and carefully checked on his grandson who was soundly asleep. The grandpa's eyes were filled with love, and his movements were quiet and slow for fear of waking up the baby. It was a seemingly ordinary scene that actually carries the weight of love and affections from an old man who had seen it all. Deng Xiaoping gazed long and deep at his grandson, while his daughter Deng Rong squatted quietly behind her father, the two savoring this touching moment together.

其乐融融

1990 年 4 月，邓小平和卓琳带着子女和小孙子在北京玉泉山享受春暖花开的美好一刻。小孙子小弟用摘下的柳树条，学着电影里的情节，编了两顶柳条帽，一顶自己戴，一顶硬是戴在了爷爷头上。全家三代人坐在一起，其乐融融。我将画面焦点集中在柳条帽上，在拍摄中使用了大胶片相机，刻意不使用闪光灯，这样可以保留自然环境中的斑驳光影，显得生动自然。

Quality Time with Family

In April 1990, Deng Xiaoping and Zhuo Lin took their children and grandson to the Yuquan Mountain in Beijing for a pleasant spring trip. Deng Xiaoping's grandson Xiao Di, as he was fondly known by his family, made two wicker hats like what he saw in a film. He placed one over his own head, and forced the other on his grandpa's head. Three generations in the Deng family were gathered together for this joyful moment. I focused my lens on the wicker hats and used a large format film camera. I refrained myself from using the flash in order to retain the natural mixture of light and shadow, so that everything looked as vivid as possible.

亲昵一吻

1992 年，时值隆冬，上海西郊宾馆外，外孙女绵绵（邓楠的孩子）亲吻爷爷的脸颊。寒冷的天气和流淌于心底的暖意定格在那一瞬间，爷爷面对这突如其来的亲吻似乎显得有点害羞。

是啊，当初那个活泼好动的小女孩如今已是亭亭玉立的大姑娘了。但在爷爷面前，她永远像个长不大的孩子，亲昵地向爷爷表达那份浓浓的爱意。

A Kiss of Love

This photo was taken outside the Xijiao State Guest Hotel in Shanghai in the cold winter of 1992. Mianmian, who is the child of Deng Xiaoping's second daughter Deng Nan, gave her grandfather a loving kiss on his cheek. Despite the freezing weather, the warm affection that flowed through Deng Xiaoping's heart was forever fixed in that moment. The grandpa seemed a bit shy about the sudden kiss.

Well, the little girl who was always alive and kicking has now grown into a young lady. But she would always be her grandpa's beloved granddaughter, who gave her grandpa a kiss filled with love.

“邓家添丁，‘82+1’，真逗！”

自从邓质方把儿子小弟带回来之后，小弟就成了家里人关注的焦点。1986年夏，家人陪伴邓小平在北戴河疗养。一天上午，小平同志偕家人一起乘车来到海滨浴场，老人家发现小弟在那里等他了，原来是保姆早早地抱着小弟来浴场等爷爷。小平同志下车，径直向小弟走去，顺手从保姆手中接过爱孙。这时，小弟本能地转动他的小脸，急着去亲爷爷，小平也高兴地做出习惯被亲吻的陶醉表情。在祖孙俩将亲未亲的一刹那，我迅速举起相机按下了快门，一幅绝妙的隔代亲情照诞生了。

等我把照片洗出来，小平既高兴又不失幽默感地故意放话：“两个丑八怪。”这一下不得了，孩子们都不同意，老人家赶紧改口：“两个噘嘴巴。”惹得众人哈哈大笑起来。老人家一锤定音：“洗出来，一家一张！”

“A New Member Added to the Deng Family, 82+1, How Interesting!”

Xiao Di, Deng Xiaoping's grandson, quickly became the focus of the family since he was brought back by his father Deng Zhifang. It was the summer of 1986 when Deng Xiaoping was taking a vacation with his family in Beidaihe. One day, just as Deng and his family arrived at the beach resort, he saw Xiao Di already waiting for him there. It turned out that the nanny had brought Deng's grandson to the resort earlier to wait for Deng's arrival. The moment Deng got off the car, he walked right towards Xiao Di and picked up his grandson from the nanny. As Xiao Di tried to give his grandpa a kiss, like he always did, Deng turned his head sideways to put on his happy face when he was being kissed. Just as this loving kiss between grandpa and grandson was about to happen, I quickly pressed the shutter to capture this magical moment filled with cross-generational love.

When I developed the photo and showed it to Deng's family, Deng Xiaoping gave a good-humored response by intentionally speaking in front of everyone, “Two ugly faces.” However, his comment backfired as the children strongly disagreed. He quickly changed his tune by saying, “Two pouty lips.” This time, his comment got everyone laughing out loud. Deng was truly satisfied with the photo and gave me an order, “Develop more photos so everyone in the family gets one!”

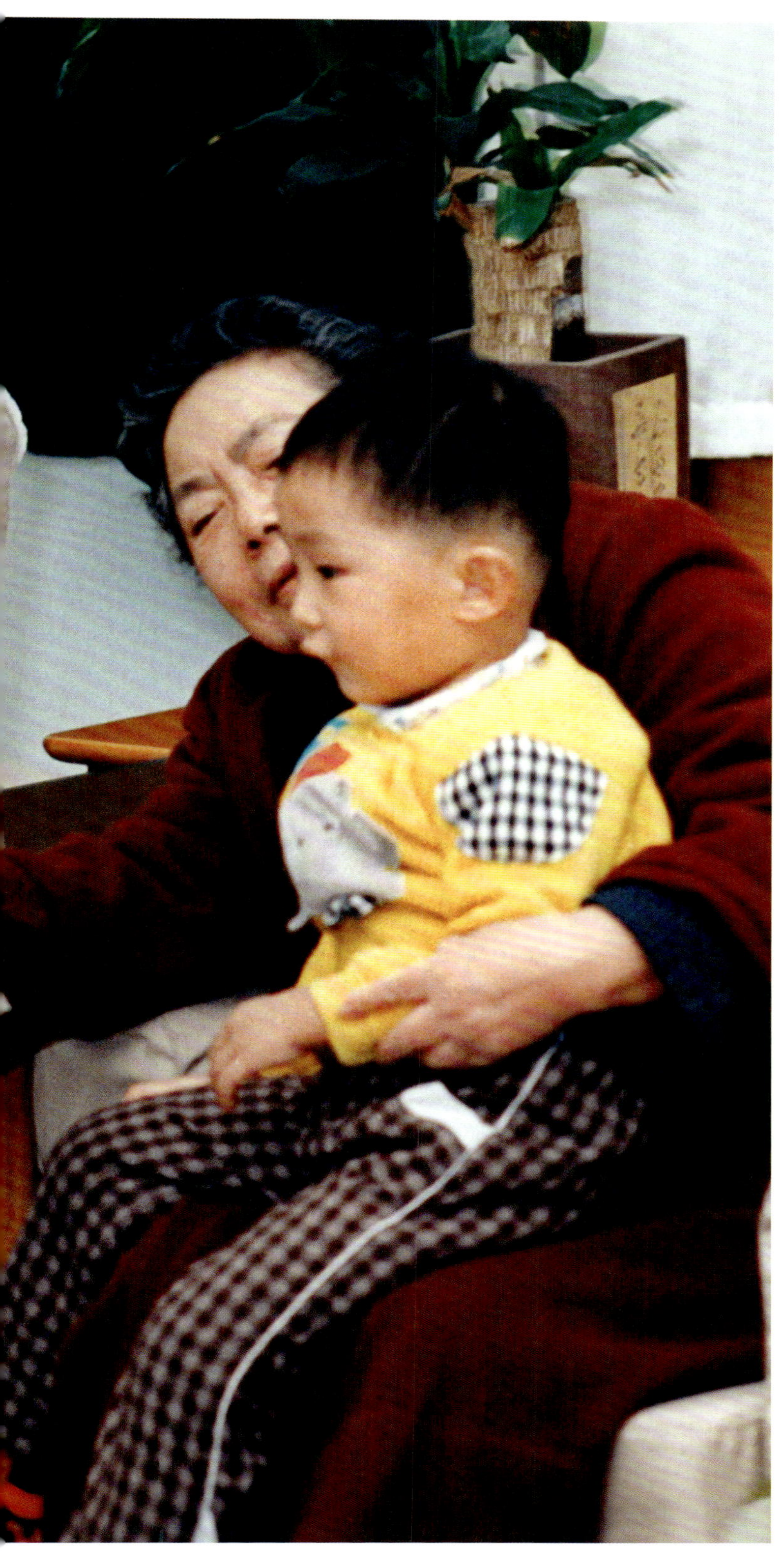

阅读习惯

1987 年，我在邓小平家里看到了温馨、和谐的一幕：小平坐在沙发上看报纸，他戴着老花镜，没穿鞋，两只脚随意地搭在前面的软凳上，很放松又很舒适的样子。孙子小弟来捣乱，闹着要让爷爷讲故事，卓琳说：“小弟，来，奶奶给你讲一个。”小弟这才安静下来。

在荷兰阿姆斯特丹与观展者交流时，我问他们为什么喜欢这幅作品，他们回答说：“因为我们在家里坐沙发也喜欢跷起腿、搭上脚，没想到邓小平也是这样。这张照片让我们看到了家庭生活中真实的邓小平。”

Reading the Newspaper at Home

This photo was taken in 1987 at Deng Xiaoping's house. It was a warm and sweet moment. Deng Xiaoping was sitting on the sofa and browsing the newspaper with his reading glasses on. Having taken off his shoes, he looked very relaxed and comfortable, as he casually crossed his legs and put them on the stool in front of him. When Xiao Di, his grandson, insisted that grandpa tell him a story, Zhuo Lin calmed the boy down by telling him a story instead.

When this photo was put on exhibition in Amsterdam, I asked the audience why they liked it so much. "Because we do the same thing at our house, you know, putting our feet up and relaxing, it never occurred to us that Deng Xiaoping, the great leader of China, was just like us", the audience replied. I guess the real attraction of this photo was because it showed all of us what Deng Xiaoping was really like at home.

爱好打桥牌

1987年，邓小平在家里打桥牌。他一手握牌，一手夹着烟，一副胸有成竹、稳操胜券的样子。女儿邓楠坐在一旁观阵，围棋大师聂卫平是小平同志的牌友，正在聚精会神地算牌。邓小平打桥牌叫牌准确，出手果断，技艺精湛，水准常令专业选手叫好。老搭档聂卫平说："他打牌守得紧、攻得狠、叫得准、打得稳，不愧为桥牌高手。"国际桥牌协会主席杨小燕也说："邓先生的牌艺是专业一流的！"

A Fan of Bridge

This photo was taken in 1987 at Deng Xiaoping's house, when he was playing bridge, his favorite pastime. The way he smoked and held his cards seemed to suggest that he knew he had a winning hand. Sitting beside Deng Xiaoping was his daughter Deng Nan, while opposite him was Nie Weiping, one of China's top Go players and Deng's longtime bridge buddy. Deng Xiaoping enjoyed a reputation for his professional competence at playing bridge, as he was accurate in counting the cards and decisive in calling them. According to Nie Weiping, his veteran bridge partner, Deng Xiaoping "plays bridge like a true master, good at both defense and offence." Yang Xiaoyan, the President of the International Bridge Association, shared the same opinion, "Mr. Deng's skills at playing bridge is without doubt first-class!"

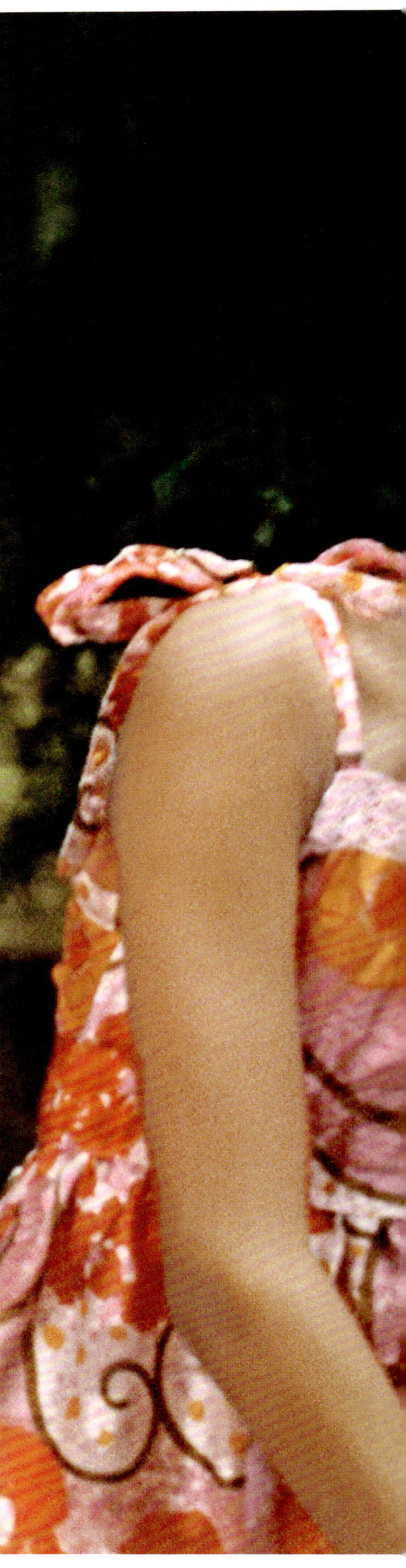

揪小辫

1985 年夏，邓小平在北戴河度假。一天，邓楠模仿新疆姑娘的发式给女儿绵绵扎了许多小辫子，碰巧让邓小平看到了，他问：“今天怎么扎了这么多小辫子？”绵绵只是嘻嘻地笑，并不答话。邓小平若有所思，不由得也笑了起来，随手揪住外孙女的小辫子，得意地说：“抓住小辫子喽！”

他肯定是想起了 1975 年领导整顿时的事情，那时“四人帮”一伙倒行逆施，疯狂围攻邓小平，企图阻止整顿的进行。在政治局会议上，邓小平说：“有人专门喜欢抓小辫子。我不怕被揪辫子，因为真理在我的手里。”此时见到外孙女头上的许多小辫子，他情不自禁地想起当年的斗争，也想起了自己说的那句话。

“Pulling the Pigtails”

This photo was taken in the summer of 1985 when Deng Xiaoping was taking a vacation in Beidaihe. One day, Deng Nan decided to weave Mianmian’s hair into pigtail braids, just like a Uyghur girl. Seeing his granddaughter’s unique hair style, Deng asked, “What’s with all these pigtails?” Mianmian simply smiled without giving an answer. Deng Xiaoping could not help but smile, as he gently pulled his granddaughter’s hair, saying cheerfully, “I got your pigtails!”

This must have brought back memories for Deng Xiaoping. When he was charged with bringing order to a chaotic China in 1975, he was frantically attacked by the unscrupulous Gang of Four, who tried desperately to sabotage Deng’s work. At one Politburo meeting, Deng Xiaoping defended himself by saying, “There are some who specialize in pulling others’ pigtails. I am not afraid of my pigtails getting pulled, because I am on the right side of history.” In Chinese politics, pulling someone’s pigtails refers to finding others’ weaknesses and faults to use as a handle for attack or blackmail. Seeing his granddaughter’s pigtail braids, Deng Xiaoping could not help but recall his own words at that meeting, and the struggles he had to endure.

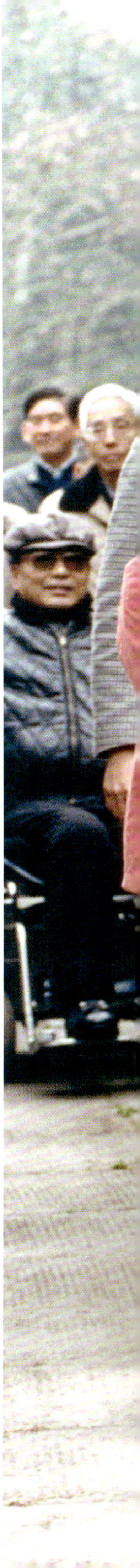

和孙辈们在一起

邓小平少小离家，戎马半生，几经沉浮起落，绝大部分精力都用在操劳国事上了。虽然儿孙满堂，平时也没有更多时间和孩子们在一起。晚年退休以后，时间宽裕多了，孙辈们终于可以整天黏在爷爷身边，邓小平也可以尽情地享受天伦之乐了。

Surrounded by His Grandchildren

Deng Xiaoping had devoted almost his entire life to the Chinese revolutionary cause. He hardly had any time to spend with his big family when he was governing the nation. Now Deng finally had the luxury to play the role of grandfather in his retirement and spend quality time with his grandchildren all day long.

墨宝流芳

邓小平同志的书法，从柳体入手，旁及黄庭坚笔意，外柔内刚，力能扛鼎，尤其细微处，斩钉截铁，点画变化莫测，气象万千，非文人书家所能企及。

Brushes with Power

Deng Xiaoping's style of Chinese calligraphy combines the artistic elements from calligraphic masters such as Liu Gongquan and Huang Tingjian from China's Tang and Song dynasties. His brushes are powerful on the inside and graceful on the outside, and decisive even in the smallest details. The changes in his strokes reflect the depth and breadth of his personality and leadership style, which dwarfs most calligraphers.

红玉兰

每一年春天来临，小平同志都要去北京西郊的玉泉山踏青。

一树娇艳动人、争相盛开的红玉兰花，在绿树黄花的背景衬托下，显得生机盎然。邓小平深受感染，情不自禁地走上前，伸手扶过一朵红玉兰，凑到鼻尖，闻一闻春天的气息。小平一副专注而陶醉的神情，丰富细腻的内心情感非常自然地流露出来，谁会想到他曾是一位叱咤风云、驰骋沙场的大将！

Sniffing the Red Magnolias

Every year when spring came, Deng Xiaoping would go to the Yuquan Mountain for an excursion in west suburban Beijing.

Surrounded by green trees and yellow flowers, the blossoming red magnolias were beaming with life. Caught in the moment, Deng Xiaoping couldn't help but reach over for a red magnolia and try to inhale the scent of spring. Who would have thought that a great revolutionary leader like Deng Xiaoping, who had fought and won numerous wars, also harbored such a sentimental side?

邓家的老祖

照片中的这位老人叫夏伯根，是小平同志的继母。在四世同堂的大家庭里，孩子们都习惯用家乡话称她为“老祖”。她是嘉陵江上贫苦船工的女儿。1950 年，重庆解放后不久，邓小平将夏伯根从老家广安接到了重庆，从此，老祖便与邓小平一家生活在一起，相互照顾，享受天伦之乐。邓小平去世后，家人继续悉心照料夏伯根，老人寿享 101 岁。

劳动人民出身的她，在小平同志起起落落的岁月里，为孩子们遮风挡雨，称得上邓家的“特等功臣”。小平同志最爱吃老祖做的家乡菜。若逢小平同志生日，她更是亲自下厨，为小平做一碗长寿面。

镜头前，皱纹爬满了这位饱经风霜的老人的脸庞，那是岁月在她脸上留下的印记，但这一切都不改她勤劳质朴又干净利落的本性。

The Great-grandmother of the Deng Family

The old woman in the photo is Xia Bogen, the stepmother of Deng Xiaoping, who was fondly called "Lao Zu" in Sichuanese (meaning great-grandmother) by the children of the Deng family. The daughter of a poor boatman on the Jialing River, she was brought from Guang'an, Deng Xiaoping's hometown, to Chongqing shortly after the city's liberation in 1950. Ever since then, Lao Zu had lived together with the Deng family, as they looked after each other through good times and bad times. After Deng Xiaoping's death, the Deng family continued to take good care of their great-grandmother, until she passed away at the age of 101.

Born into a working people's family, Xia Bogen devoted herself to protecting and taking care of Deng Xiaoping's children when he was going through political ups and downs. Her special contribution to the Deng family was highly approved. Whenever it was Deng Xiaoping's birthday, Lao Zu would personally cook a bowl of longevity noodles for him, who always enjoyed the hometown-flavor dishes she cooked.

As seen from this photo, Lao Zu's face was full of wrinkles, and they were marks of the ages. Despite all the challenges and difficulties that she had to endure with, Lao Zu always remained true to herself as a hardworking, clean and simple person.

北戴河避暑

邓小平在北戴河的度假生活平静而多彩。他不喜欢在室内游泳池游泳，不管天气好坏，每天都要在大海里游一个小时。他说：“我的身体还好，头脑还清楚，记忆力还不错。”在日常生活中，他一直保持老百姓的日常生活习惯，嗑点儿瓜子，抿口黄酒，时常吃一吃继母夏伯根老人亲手做的家乡面条。在医生和孩子们的建议下，他的烟也抽得少了，后来索性戒掉。为中国人民奋斗了一辈子的小平，终于能静下心来，好好享受一下安逸舒适的晚年生活。

Summer Vacation in Beidaihe

Deng Xiaoping's vacation time in Beidaihe was quiet yet colorful. Not one for the comfort of indoor swimming pools, he would swim for one hour in the sea as his daily practice, no matter the weather conditions. He used to say, "My body is healthy, my mind still works, and I still have a good memory." He had always kept the habits of ordinary people, such as chewing sunflower seeds, drinking Chinese yellow wine, and eating hometown noodles cooked by his stepmother, Xia Bogen. Following suggestions from the doctor and his children, he gradually quit smoking. After a lifetime of serving the Chinese people, Deng Xiaoping finally had the time to truly relax and enjoy his retirement.

相濡以沫——小平夫妇和邓朴方夫妇的合影

邓小平与卓琳患难与共，相守一生。邓小平之所以能为中国革命和建设事业做出杰出贡献，从容面对历次政治风云变幻，与他有一个温暖、幸福的家，有一位温柔、善良、在背后默默支持和奉献的妻子是分不开的。小平夫妇疼爱儿女，对在“文革”中被迫害致残的长子邓朴方更多一份怜爱。他们用深沉的爱去抚平儿子心灵和肉体上的创伤。

1992 年冬，小平夫妇和邓朴方夫妇在上海西郊宾馆合影留念。

Love and Care in the Family——Deng Xiaoping and His Wife Zhuo Lin, with Their Son Deng Pufang and His Wife

Deng Xiaoping and Zhuo Lin had been through thick and thin together in their entire life. Deng's great contributions to China's revolutionary cause and development would not have been possible without the selfless support and sacrifice made by his loving wife, who was always there for him even when he reached the nadir of his political career. Deng Xiaoping and his wife loved their children whole-heartedly, while they had special affections for their eldest son, Deng Pufang, who was persecuted and became disabled during the Cultural Revolution. They tried to heal their son's physical and mental wounds with their deep love.

This photo of Deng Xiaoping's family, including Zhuo Lin, their son Deng Pufang and his wife, was taken in the winter of 1992 at the Xijiao State Guest Hotel in Shanghai.

入乡随俗

1991 年 2 月，小平同志视察上海，下榻在西郊宾馆。初春的江南气温还是很低，怕老人家受冻，女儿们专门为父亲买了一件上海老人常穿的大棉袄。小平同志入乡随俗，高兴地穿在身上。

Doing as the Locals Do

The weather was pretty chilly in early spring when Deng Xiaoping stayed at the Xijiao State Guest Hotel during his visit to Shanghai in February 1991. Afraid that the old man would catch a cold, Deng Xiaoping's children bought a cotton coat for him. It was the kind of cotton coats that old people in Shanghai would often wear in cold winter. "Doing as the locals do", Deng Xiaoping happily put on the coat.

春游

每逢周末或假期，邓小平和家人喜欢到北京附近的公园里散步和赏花。到稍远的地方，老人家也不忘带着一家老小，共享家庭的和谐与幸福。这是 1986 年夏天，邓小平全家在北京玉泉山游览时的合影。画面上自左至右：邓楠、绵绵、羊羊、邓小平、小弟、萌萌、卓琳、邓林、继母夏伯根、邓先芙。

Family Trip

On weekends or holidays, Deng Xiaoping and his family liked to take walks and enjoy the scenery in the parks around Beijing. When Deng had to take a long-distance trip, he would always take his family with him so they could spend more time together. This photo was taken in the summer of 1986, when Deng Xiaoping and his family were touring the Yuquan Mountain in Beijing.

From left to right: Deng Nan, Mianmian, Yangyang, Deng Xiaoping, Xiaodi, Mengmeng, Zhuo Lin, Deng Lin, Deng Xiaoping's stepmother Xia Bogen, Deng Xianfu.

和毛主席在一起

1965 年春节，父亲杨尚昆告诉我："今晚在北京饭店有会餐，毛主席会到，你也参加，一起去吧。"听到这个消息，想到今晚就能见到许久不见的毛伯伯，我一直兴奋得无法平静。来到餐厅，我一眼就看到毛伯伯和邓伯伯坐在沙发上谈天，还没来得及上前问候，没想到毛主席大声说："小二来啦！"并欠起身和我握手。这真是让我受宠若惊。从延安开始，毛伯伯就一直这样关心我。

合影趣事

1989 年 8 月 22 日，是邓小平 85 岁寿辰。我带着几名助手，来到北戴河寓所为老人家拍摄纪念照。

拍完照，正当我们收拾器材准备离开时，卓琳阿姨把我叫住："小二别走，你还没和我们俩合影呢！"我回头一看，只见两位老人已经坐在藤椅上等我了。我很是兴奋，赶忙跑到他们身后，准备拍照。邓伯伯看着我说："站到后边做啥子，就在前边坐嘛！"我高兴地坐在二位老人家膝前，正准备拍照时突然觉得头发被人捏住了，没等我回头，助手孙贵成已经按下了快门。

回到北京，我把照片冲印出来一看，原来是卓琳阿姨别出心裁，捏住了我的一绺头发。我把照片拿回来，众人皆赞："数这张照片最新颖。"

Shaking Hands with Chairman Mao

During the Spring Festival of 1965, my father Yang Shangkun told me, "Tonight there will be a dinner party at the Beijing Hotel. Chairman Mao will be there, and you can come as well." I was really thrilled about the opportunity to meet Chairman Mao that night, because I hadn't seen him in person for a while. The moment I walked into the dining room, I saw Uncle Mao and Uncle Deng (Deng Xiaoping) chatting on the sofa. Before I had the chance to say hello to them, Chairman Mao shouted at me, "There you are, Xiao Er!", and stood up to shake my hands. Xiao Er was my nickname, and I was truly flattered by Chairman Mao's friendly gesture. Uncle Mao had always cared about me since I was a little boy in Yan'an.

The Story Behind a Photo

August 22, 1989 was Deng Xiaoping's 85th birthday. To commemorate this special occasion, I took a few assistants with me to Beidaihe to take photos for him.

Just as I was packing up and ready to leave after taking the pictures, Aunt Zhuo Lin called me back, "Xiao Er, don't go so fast, you haven't taken a photo with us!" I turned around and saw Uncle Deng and Aunt Zhuo Lin already sitting down on their rattan armchairs and waiting for me. Feeling truly excited, I rushed behind them and got ready for the picture. Uncle Deng then said to me, "What are you doing in the back, come and sit in the front!" And I happily obliged and sat down right in front of them. All of a sudden, I felt someone was pulling my hair. Before I could turn around, my assistant Sun Guicheng had already pressed the shutter.

When I had the photo developed, I discovered that it was Aunt Zhuo Lin who was pinching my hair without giving me prior notice. As I showed the photo to everyone, they all applauded its originality.

1988 年，杨绍明拍摄的《退下来以后的邓小平》获得荷兰第 31 届世界新闻摄影大赛新闻人物类组照三等奖，成为首位获得该奖的中国摄影师，这是他在获奖作品的展板前的留影。

Yang Shaoming won third prize in the People in the News category in the 1988 World Press Photo Contest with his photo series "Deng Xiaoping in His Retirement", becoming the first photographer from China to win a WPP award. This picture shows him commemorating the moment in front of the exhibition of his award-winning photos.

作者简历

杨绍明，1942 年出生，汉族，中共党员。杨尚昆之子。1966 年毕业于北京大学历史系，大学学历，为中国当代著名摄影家、新华社高级记者。曾任中国国际友谊促进会副会长、中国宋庆龄基金会副主席、中央文献研究室邓小平生平著作研究组副组长、中国摄影家学会副主席及分党组成员。曾创建中国当代摄影学会并担任主席，创建世界华人摄影学会并当选为会长。1980 年，杨绍明踏访了红军先辈们走过的长征路，首次编辑出版了个人画集《雪山草地行》，叶剑英元帅为画册封面题词。

About the Editor

Yang Shaoming was born in 1942 and is the son of Yang Shangkun. He is of the Han ethnicity and a member of the Communist Party of China. After graduating from Peking University in 1966 with a Bachelor's degree, he had worked as a senior photojournalist for Xinhua News Agency. Since then, he had held numerous positions such as Vice President of the China Association for Friendship, Vice President of the China Soong Ching Ling Foundation, Deputy Director of the Research Department of Deng Xiaoping's Life and Works under the Party Literature Research Center of the CPC Central Committee, and Vice President of the China Photographers Association as well as Member of CPA's Leading Party Group. Yang Shaoming is widely recognized as one of modern China's most accomplished and influential photographers. He was the founding chairman of the China Modern Photographers Association, and the founding president of the Society of Worldwide Ethnic Chinese Photographers. After retracing the footsteps of the forefathers of the Chinese Red Army, he edited and published his debut photo album titled Journey to the Snowy Mountains and the Grasslands in 1980. Ye Jianying, the renowned Chinese communist revolutionary and military leader, inscribed the book's front cover for him.

策　　划：杨绍明　管慧勇　奚天鹰

主　　编：杨绍明

副 主 编：管慧勇　朱大路　李　芳
编 辑 组：闫　伟　闫　鹏
撰　　文：李华强　刘　刊　荣　毅　刘　文
英文顾问：唐闻生
英文翻译：张国玺

图书在版编目（CIP）数据

点亮：一位摄影师眼中的邓小平 / 杨绍明编著. -- 杭州：浙江人民美术出版社, 2021.8

ISBN 978-7-5340-8977-0

Ⅰ. ①点… Ⅱ. ①杨… Ⅲ. ①邓小平（1904-1997）—生平事迹—摄影集 Ⅳ. ①A762-64

中国版本图书馆CIP数据核字（2021）第168106号

策划编辑：奚天鹰
责任编辑：王　铭
文字编辑：黄　静
装帧设计：王　铭　钱　伟
责任校对：余雅汝　毛依依
责任印制：陈柏荣

点亮——一位摄影师眼中的邓小平

杨绍明　编著

出版发行：浙江人民美术出版社
（杭州市体育场路347号）
经　　销：全国各地新华书店
制　　版：浙江新华图文制作有限公司
印　　刷：浙江影天印业有限公司
版　　次：2021年8月第1版
印　　次：2021年8月第1次印刷
开　　本：965mm×1270mm　1/16
印　　张：12
字　　数：139千字
印　　数：0,001—1,500
书　　号：ISBN 978-7-5340-8977-0
定　　价：280.00元